IMAGES
of America
THE HOUSE OF DAVID
BASEBALL TEAM

IMAGES
of America

THE HOUSE OF DAVID

BASEBALL TEAM

Joel Hawkins and Terry Bertolino

ISBN 0-7385-0759-0

Published by Arcadia Publishing
Charleston SC, Chicago IL, Portsmouth NH, San Francisco CA

Printed in the United States of America

Library of Congress Catalog Card Number: 00106070

For all general information contact Arcadia Publishing at:
Telephone 843-853-2070
Fax 843-853-0044
E-mail sales@arcadiapublishing.com
For customer service and orders:
Toll-Free 1-888-313-2665

Visit us on the Internet at www.arcadiapublishing.com

DEDICATION

To my wife, Martine, who has put up with more than most wives should have to, and also to my son, Zach, "The Boy," who I consider to be my good luck charm.

—Joel

I would like to pay homage to my wife, Effrosine, and my daughter, Athena, for having such great names…and for putting up with me through all of this.

—Terry

Contents

Acknowledgments

We would like to give an extra thank you to the following people for their time and help in the development of this project: Ron Taylor, Secretary of the City of David, curator of their museum, and the author of *Mary's City of David*, for his assistance and loan of photos that were used in this work; Lloyd Dalager, President of the House of David, for his stories, time, photos, and information that led to the identification of many of the people in our photos; George and Exa Anderson for their many photos, shared memories, and anecdotes that helped us get over many of the bumps in the road we encountered; and Ron Kronewitter for his photos, many of which were used to fill in gaps that were present in our work.

We would also like to thank the following people for their help, input, or inspiration: Glenn Uminowicz and Bob Myers, from the Berrien County Historical Association, for the promotion and help that they gave us; and Jill Rauh, of the Benton Harbor Public Library, for the use of photos and access to the photographic collection at their House of David Room. Also Henry and Jean Thole for their assistance, Chris Cook for his help in locating a publisher, Wayne Stivers for use of his photographs, Marc King for his enthusiasm, and Terry Cannon for introducing us.

In addition, thank you to all of those people who contacted our webpage and submitted or donated information to our project: Tony Zitta, Chet Bush, William Cross, Rochelle Busch, Gary Dacus, Kelly Johnson, Judith Ann Hall Foster, Evan Morgan, Norm Synder, Steve Wulff, Lila Blake, Richard Bennett, Bill Schnarre, Eddie Deal, Vernon Smith, Fred Larson, Mel and Millie Atwell, Gretchen Brosius, Dick Hummel, Lew Hummel, Paul Jarvis, Tim Henville, Robert Utely, Elsie Nusser, Judie Nusser, Ike Bohn, Harvey Pallas, Pete Sandman, John Pavlick, Lyle K. Wilson, Thomas H. Smith, Mike Chozen, Roy Alexander, Tony Mangiere, Andy Calise, Bill Swank, Robert Karstens, and Howard Crossman.

—Joel and Terry

I would first like to thank my partner, Terry Bertolino, for pushing me to get this idea into a completed project. In addition, I would like to thank the following people for their help, ideas, inspiration, or just their support: Jay Dahl and all the people at Perfect Image for their great help in photographic restoration and duplication, many of which are used in this project. Also, Clare Adkin, author of *Brother Benjamin*, for his original inspiration, Keith Tucker for the donation of his father's scrapbooks and baseball photo collection, and to all my friends and family who kept asking and encouraging me to complete this project.

—Joel

I would like to thank my partner, Joel Hawkins, for taking me on board and allowing me to share in his initial vision. I would also like to thank Larry McCay (Larry McCay Photography, Inc.), whose help with picture development was invaluable, Jon Biek, for the phone call that started it all, Meg Sundell, Beth Hemmer, and my parents, without whom none of this would have been possible.

—Terry

INTRODUCTION

The House of David is a religious colony founded in 1903 by Benjamin and Mary Purnell and located in Benton Harbor, Michigan. Though small in number, their accomplishments were many. They were strong contributors to the agricultural community around them. It is thought that they developed one of the first cold storage facilities in the country and were the first to preserve jellies in jars. As early as 1908, they established a pre-Disney type amusement park, complete with miniature trains. A zoo and aviary were soon added to the park. They were also credited with inventing the automatic pinsetter used in their bowling alley. One of the tenets of their faith was vegetarianism, and the colony restaurant, serving original-recipe vegetarian meals, was credited with producing the first "sugar cone." They built a three-story hotel in downtown Benton Harbor and an elaborate motor lodge, "The Grand Vista," south of town. They built tourist cabins, bottled water from their own natural springs, erected a synagogue for their Jewish friends, and for a brief period of time even had an "on-site" hospital. They constructed a large amphitheater to accommodate their accomplished orchestra and world-renowned jazz band. They had a complete logging operation on High Island in northern Michigan. Another tenet of their faith was that they must neither shave nor cut their hair. When a few of the colony members were refused employment with a local streetcar company because of their appearance, the House of David bought controlling interest in the firm and soon all conductors were seen with long hair and beards!

The feature for which the House of David is perhaps best remembered, however, is the talented teams of bearded barnstorming baseball players that traveled to nearly every state in the Union, Mexico, and most of the Canadian Provinces. Early in the team's history, when their travels took them primarily to the east, their competition would often consist of the formidable Negro League teams: the Pittsburgh Crawfords, the Bacharach Giants, the Newark Eagles, and the Homestead Grays. Later in the 1930s, both the House of David and the City of David would barnstorm across the country with the Kansas City Monarchs. In 1939, the City of David hooked up with Satchel Paige's All Stars for over two months, playing 60 games between them.

Grover Cleveland Alexander would serve as manager/pitcher for one of the House of David teams from 1931 through 1935. Chief Bender was also a member of the 1933 eastern traveling team, along with Jackie Mitchell, the first woman to ever sign a professional baseball contract. In 1934, Babe Didrikson Zaharais joined the Eastern traveling team. That same year also saw one of the first integrated teams take the field when Satchel Paige and Cy Perkins, his catcher, signed on to play with the Davids in the Denver Post tournament. As late as the mid-1950s, the City of David was still barnstorming with Paige, now with the Harlem Globetrotters.

The House of David is credited with inventing the "Pepper Game." Doc Tally, John Tucker, and Dutch Faust are thought to have originated it, with George Anderson replacing Faust when he left and helping to raise its level to the point where it was often billed as an attraction that was as entertaining as the game itself. The House of David ballpark was built around 1910 to accommodate the Fitzsimmons Speed Boys, a local semi-pro team. When they were out of town, the Colony used the diamond to play neighboring school teams. In 1914, Doc Tally, with the help of his two brothers and Francis Thorpe, formed what is thought to be the first officially uniformed team. In 1916, they won the Berrien County championship, and news of their prowess began to spread.

An article by the Associated News Service appeared in 1919 about the team, and in 1920 they were featured in a *New York Times* mid-week pictorial.

All was well, with only one House of David traveling team on the road, until an internal struggle tore the Colony in two. In 1930, the Mary's City of David formed, and with its formation came the "second" House of David traveling baseball team. Both the City of David and the House of David claimed to be the "original" ball club. By 1934, there were as many as four Benton Harbor teams on the road. The City of David, which had no home park, was destined to be forever the "visitors," while the House of David sent out an Eastern, Western, and Central States traveling team and also utilized the "home" diamond. To add to the confusion, Louis Murphy, a former House of David promoter, formed his own House of David team, complete with whiskers, and played primarily in the Southeast.

The last year the House of David sent out a true "traveling" team was in 1936; the City of David continued on the road until 1956. The House of David joined the three-I league, c. 1940, and continued to play locally. Both teams suspended baseball operation during the War, 1941–1945, with the City reforming their traveling team in 1946 and the House continuing to play on weekends for a brief period of time.

We hope that this pictorial history will enable you to get a small glimpse into the life of one of the most entertaining and remarkable barnstorming baseball teams to ever criss-cross this great continent of ours. Enjoy the journey.

One

1914–1920

In the Beginning

On April 3, 1903, Benjamin Purnell, an itinerate preacher, along with his wife Mary, created the Israelite House of David, a religious colony, in Benton Harbor, Michigan, with land donated by devote followers. Within a few years, the colony had close to five hundred members living on the colony grounds.

After creating a "pick-up"-type baseball team, the House of David organized a traditional baseball team in the spring of 1915, which progressed into a money-making endeavor for the 1915 season. Francis Thorpe was named manager. This is the first known photograph of the team. They are, from left to right: (seated) Ruben Jaft, Ezra "Cookie" Hannaford, Richard Marcum, Curtis ?, Barlow Tally; (standing) Frank Hornbeck, Horace Hannaford, unidentified, Swaney Tally, Francis Thorpe, Paul Mooney, J.L. "Doc" Tally, Frank Wyland, Monroe Wulff. Benjamin Purnell is on the far left.

As the colony grew, they built an amusement park and eventually a baseball field, which was used by a local semi-pro team. The House of David boys used this field when it was empty. By 1914, the attraction of a long-haired, bearded team was gaining the interest of local citizens, who came out and watched them play.

In 1916, with Francis Thorpe in only his second season of managerial duty, the House of David Baseball Team won the Berrien County Championship. They are, from left to right: (front row) Glenn Klum and Swaney Tally; (middle row) Barlow Tally, Horace Hannaford, Frank Hornbeck, Austin "Tex" Williams, and Francis Thorpe; (back row) Jerry Hansel, Frank Wyland, Paul Mooney, Ezra "Cookie" Hannaford, and Jessie Lee "Doc" Tally.

At the start of the 1917 season, the House of David joined the Inter-City Baseball Association of Chicago. In joining this league they were able to expand their schedule and play teams in southwest Michigan, northern Indiana, and, of course, Chicago. At the end of the season the House of David ended up with a league record of 17 wins and only 13 losses.

The House of David baseball field, located on the colony grounds, was a hitter's paradise. The distance down the left field line was only 257 feet, and the right field distance of 222 feet favored left-handed power-hitters like Doc Tally. In 1917, he hit four homeruns in 29 games, which might seem low, but the Major League record for the same year was only 12 in 154 games.

Lloyd Dalager was once asked, "Was it a nice place to play?" to which he replied, "Oh,...seemed to be. Attract quite a (crowd). Kind of open, you know. The young guys...they want to get out there, just crack a few homers, and stuff like that, you know. No restrictions."

This 1918 photograph of the baseball team was taken on the House of David colony grounds at Eden Springs. It should be noted that the entire team pictured was comprised solely of House of David members. They are, from left to right: (seated) Charlie Falkenstein, Artie Vieritz, and Austin "Tex" Williams; (standing) Glenn Klum, Ezra "Cookie" Hannaford, Hubert "Hip" Vaughn, Frank Hornbeck, Doc Tally, Manager Francis Thorpe, Paul Mooney, Horace Hannaford, Frank Wyland, and Jerry Hansel.

The 1919 House of David Girls Baseball Team was thought to be the best girl's team of the colony, having gone undefeated during the 1919 season. Playing against teams such as the Chicago Colored Girls and the Chicago All-American Ladies Team, the House of David girls handily beat them, as well as all comers. One reason might be that six of the team members were actually men. Once asked why he would wear a dress and play, House of David second baseman, Zeke Bauschke replied, "It was a chance to play!" Zeke caught, while his friend, Luther Jackson, pitched for the team. You will notice many of the same last names as House of David regular players. They are, from left to right: (seated) Marie Falkenstein, Marge Vieritz, Frieda Falkenstein, May Vaughn, and Helen Smith; (standing) Arthur Jackson, Dwight "Zeke" Bauschke, Marietta Smith, Jewell Boone, Dave Harrison, Elijah Burland, Mildred Vaughn, Oscar Sassman, and Luther Jackson.

Opposite: Although Francis Thorpe is pictured here, it is doubtful that this was little more than a photo opportunity for the remaining colony members. Team shots were a popular subject for House of David postcards. They are, from left to right: (seated) Jim Moor, Francis Thorpe, and Estelle Hornbeck; (standing) John Bulley, Benny Hill, Wesley Snyder, Joseph Bulley, Edmond Bulley, and Tom Atkins.

In a three hour, 19-inning game, the House of David nine defeated the LaPorte All Stars by a score of 1–0. The game was played on the House of David diamond. Never in the history of the House of David ball teams had there been a diamond battle that had gone 18 innings without a counter going over home plate. A capacity crowd witnessed the game.

"Jewel Boone was one of the best pitchers on the girls team. One time she came walking by when we were running on the train. We were playing catch in back of the depot there, another guy and I. She wanted to throw. Boy, she could throw that old ball pretty good yet...she could log it! That was probably 20 to 30 years after she played ball, you know." (Interview with Lloyd Dalager.)

The 1920 House of David Home Team is pictured above. Percy Walker and Wesley Schneider both managed the home teams. They are, from left to right: (kneeling) Dwight "Zeke" Bauschke, Stan Bell, Frank Wyland, Wesley Schneider, Jerry Hansel, Elijah Burkland, and unidentified; (standing) Bert Johnson, Cyril "Mickey" McFarland, Manna Woodworth, Paul Mooney, Percy Walker, Harvey Bauschke, and Hiram Croft.

Here we see Gatemen Bill Frye and Hans Dalager showing one of the ways they promoted themselves while on the road. Bill Frye was the team's representative for ticket receipts. His other responsibility was taking care of advertising, which he did by selling postcards and spreading the word about the House of David colony.

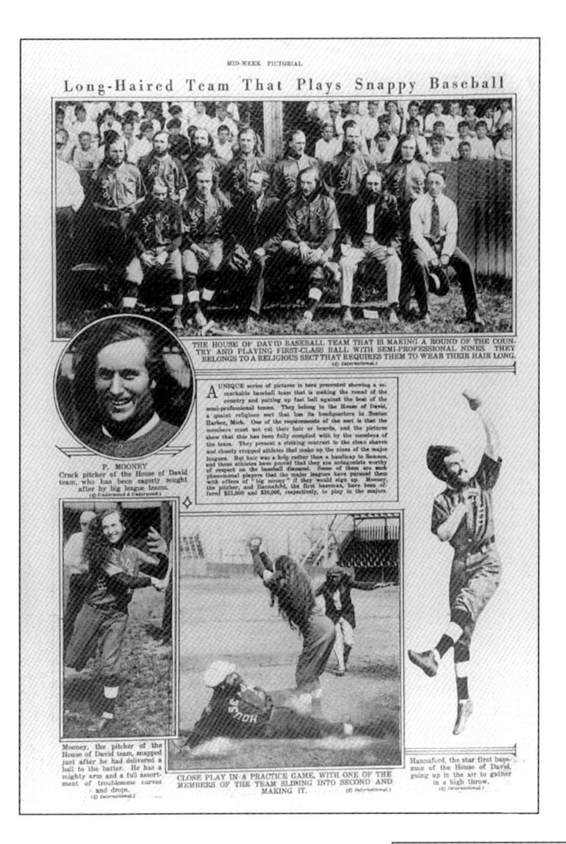

MID-WEEK PICTORIAL

Long-Haired Team That Plays Snappy Baseball

THE HOUSE OF DAVID BASEBALL TEAM THAT IS MAKING A ROUND OF THE COUNTRY AND PLAYING FIRST-CLASS BALL WITH SEMI-PROFESSIONAL NINES. THEY BELONGS TO A RELIGIOUS SECT THAT REQUIRES THEM TO WEAR THEIR HAIR LONG. (© International.)

P. MOONEY
Crack pitcher of the House of David team, who has been eagerly sought after by big league teams. (© Underwood & Underwood.)

A UNIQUE series of pictures is here presented showing a remarkable baseball team that is making the round of the country and putting up fast ball against the best of the semi-professional teams. They belong to the House of David, a quaint religious sect that has its headquarters in Benton Harbor, Mich. One of the requirements of the sect is that the members must not cut their hair or beards, and the pictures show that this has been fully complied with by the members of the team. They present a striking contrast to the clean shaven and closely cropped athletes that make up the nines of the major leagues. But hair was a help rather than a handicap to Samson, and these athletes have proved that they are antagonists worthy of respect on the baseball diamond. Some of them are such phenomenal players that the major leagues have pursued them with offers of "big money" if they would sign up. Mooney, the pitcher, and Hannaford, the first baseman, have been offered $25,000 and $30,000, respectively, to play in the majors.

Mooney, the pitcher of the House of David team, snapped just after he had delivered a ball to the batter. He has a mighty arm and a full assortment of troublesome curves and drops. (© International.)

CLOSE PLAY IN A PRACTICE GAME, WITH ONE OF THE MEMBERS OF THE TEAM SLIDING INTO SECOND AND MAKING IT. (© International.)

Hannaford, the star first baseman of the House of David, going up in the air to gather in a high throw. (© International.)

Evidence of the early popularity of the House of David team can be found in a 1920 issue of the *Mid-Week Pictorial*, which stated that "the team is making a round of the country and playing first-class ball with semi-pro nines." Under the circular photo of Paul Mooney reads, "Crack picture of the House of David, who has been eagerly sought after by big league teams." The caption is correct; unfortunately the picture is actually Hipp Vaughn.

LONG-HAIRED PITCHER SOUGHT BY CUBS

The House of David, a religious sect colonized in Michigan, produced this remarkable ball team. They sure do look like the original bush leaguers. Mooney, their star pitcher (fifth from the left) has learned how to "curl 'em over" so well that the Cubs want him in Chicago. It's plain to see these boys are easy winners—they never had a close shave yet.

The House of David attracted many talented people, and many used their talents to help the colony. Baseball players Glenn Klum, Charlie Falkenstein, Horace Hannaford, and Ezra Hannaford also played in the traveling band. Pictured here is the 1920 House of David Traveling Team. Seated is Francis Thorpe. They are, from left to right: Glenn Klum, Artie Veritz, Austin "Tex" Williams, Ezra "Cookie" Hannaford, Paul Mooney, Jerry Hansel, Frank Wyland, Hubert "Hip" Vaughn, Horace Hannford, Charlie Falkenstein, and Jesse Lee "Doc" Tally.

Two

1921–1928

The Formative Years

This is a popular photograph that was used in both poster and postcard form to advertise the House of David baseball team in the early 1920s. This picture is often misidentified as the "Pepper Team," or early 1900 House of David ballplayers. The players are, from left to right: Hubert "Hip" Vaughn, Walter "Dutch" Faust, and Horace Hannaford. This Hip Vaughn is not the same one who pitched for the Chicago Cubs from 1913 to 1921.

Similar to the Negro Leagues, the House of David would spend weeks, even months, on the road. In some cases, they would play two games a day in different locations. Along the way from one to the other, they would stop and eat. Taking the seats out of the cars, they would sit together in groups that they called "broom handles." This was a time to talk and discuss strategy for upcoming games.

"Bill Frye (right) never threw a baseball in his life. Frye sold postcards and literature among the crowd during the game. He was kinda' the comedian too. People would ask, how do you grow a beard like that? Well, you've got to get the right kind of fertilizer, he'd reply. Anything to give them an answer. You'd hear people laughing and you knew Frye was around." (Interview with Lloyd Dalager.)

The start of the 1922 House of David season saw some new faces on the Traveling Team. This was thanks in part to the built-in farm system they developed. New to this team were future stars Dutch Faust, Zeke Bauschke, and Les Bell. Pictured here, from left to right, are: Walter "Dutch" Faust, Jesse Lee "Doc" Tally, Austin "Tex" Williams, Paul Mooney, Ezra "Cookie" Hannford, Frank Wyland, Hubert "Hip" Vaughn, Horace Hannaford, Francis Thorpe, Charlie Falkenstein, Artie Veritz, Les Bell, and Dwight "Zeke" Bauschke.

Breaking in together with the Traveling Team, Walter "Dutch" Faust (left) and Dwight "Zeke" Bauschke (right) were given the moniker of "Diamond Cutters" for their prowess in turning double plays during the 1922 and 1923 seasons. Neither of them had played baseball before becoming House of David members.

Taken on the Colony grounds, this photo features seven members of the House of David baseball team. In the background are two of the tourist cabins that were also a popular attraction for summer visitors. Left to right are: Hans "Barney" Dalager, Dave "Eggs" Harrison, William Frye, Francis Thorpe, John Tucker, B.D. "Red" Smith, and Jesse Lee "Doc" Tally.

This photograph of the 1925 House of David Traveling Team was taken in Sioux City, Iowa. By the beginning of the next year, Dutch Faust would leave the team to report to the Texas League. Pictured here are, from left to right: (kneeling) Dave "Eggs" Harriåson, ? Curtis, Harold "Pup" Smith, Jesse Lee "Doc" Tally, A.B. Hipp, and Walter "Dutch" Faust; (standing) ? Sharrock, Bill Heckman, ? Lane, John Tucker, Bill Frye, Lloyd Miller, ? Champion, and Ed "Koke" Coykendall.

On March 4, 1926, Israelite member Walter "Dutch" Faust signed a contract to play for the Dallas Steers of the Texas Association. Dutch was the only true member of the House of David to sign a contract to play professional baseball. In two years of professional baseball Dutch did not move past the "A" level, and retired due to injuries.

This photograph was taken April 23, 1927, and has a caption written by Hans Dalager that reads: "Crossing the swollen Illinois river on a ferry. We had 3 cars go on the ferry but could not get them all on the picture—we are 17 men traveling." Pictured are Dave Harrison, Hans Dalager, and John Tucker.

Taken on the House of David baseball team's home field, it shows a Home Team from the 1927–1928 period. They are, from left to right: Billy Edmonds, Lionel Everett, Horace Hannaford, B.D. "Red" Smith, Miles Crow, Frank Wyland, Wesley Snyder, Tom Dewhirst, Percy Walker, Bob Dewhirst, Ezra "Cookie" Hannaford, George Anderson, and Clay "Mud" Williams.

This is the 1927 Junior team, photographed at the colony park. Seated is Dave Harrison, House of David Traveling Team member and coach of the Junior squad. Pictured from left to right are: Jimmie Crow, Hobie Nelson, Glendon "Red" Wiltbank, Billy Link, Ernie Selby, George Anderson, Lionel Everett, Jack Crow, Earl Boyersmith, Sidney Smith, and Leo "Lefty" Wiltbank.

This photograph was taken at Trenton, Rhode Island, August 7, 1927, when the House of David played the Philadelphia Giants in front of between three and four thousand people. When traveling east in the '20s, the House of David often scheduled games with various Negro League teams. Zeke Bauschke remembered games against the Homestead Grays, the Bacharach Giants, and the Indianapolis ABCs. When asked how they fared he replied, "Most of the time they knocked our ears off!"

After a long and disabling illness, Israelite House of David leader, Benjamin Purnell, died on December 16, 1927, at the age of 66. Some contend that the prolonged court cases and his persecution by the media caused his death.

Beginning on March 11, 1928, the House of David played 172 games for the season. Their record was a very respectable 110 wins, 56 losses, and 6 ties. Players are, from left to right: (sitting) A.V. "Rip" Atherton, Roy "Old Folks" Blackmore, Joe Gilmore, "Bud" Zediker, Jesse Lee "Doc" Tally, and Joe "Windy" Radloff; (standing) Francis Thorpe, George "Lefty" Gilbert, A.B. Hipp, John Tucker, B.D. "Red" Smith, Page Neve, Clifford Reed, Carl "Cyclone" Pederson, and Ed "Koke" Coykendall.

Pictured here are members of the 1928 House of David Home Team. This photo was taken in the right field area of the House of David ballpark, which was located just outside of the Edens Springs Amusement Park. They are, from left to right: (front row) Clay "Mud" Williams, Horace Hannaford, and George Anderson; (back row) Dave "Eggs" Harrison, Percy Walker, Tom Dewhirst, and Bob Dewhirst.

The 1928 House of David Traveling Team photographed in Spokane, WA, June 10, 1928. The members are sitting on the front of the new Hudson Super Six Sedan that John Tucker had just received the day before. They are, from left to right: (seated) A.V. "Rip" Atherton, Roy "Old Folks" Blackmore, and Joe Gilmore; (standing) B. D. "Red" Smith, George "Lefty" Gilbert, Carl "Cyclone" Pederson, A.B. Hipp, Joe "Windy" Radloff, John Tucker, Clifford Reed, Page Neve, Francis Thorpe, and Ed "Koke" Coykendall.

The 1928 House of David pitching staff is pictured above. This group had a combined record of 60–32, against teams such as Milwaukee of the American Association, the Dallas Steers of the Texas League, the Fresno Tigers, the Gilkerson Union Giants, and the Spencer Cubs. From left to right, with pitching records, are: ? Gebo—7–4, Page Neve—18–8, George "Lefty" Gilbert—13–12, Fred "Joe" Radloff—19–8, and Jesse Lee "Doc" Tally—3–0.

Francis Thorpe had many successes as Business Manager and Financial Secretary at both the House of David and later at the City of David. Unfortunately, his team of "vertically impaired" ballplayers was not among them. It is uncertain if this team ever got off the ground, or actually played a ball game. You could say this particular venture of Francis's was very short-lived!

The 1928 team won the Berrien County and Southwest Michigan Championships. This was the last team picture before the division of the colony. They are, from left to right: (kneeling) Mason "Mac" Perry, Al Stem, George Anderson, and Walter "Dutch" Faust; (standing) Percy Walker, Bob Dewhirst, Tom Dewhirst, John Tucker, Miles Crow, Bert Johnson, Dave "Eggs" Harrison, and Frank Wyland. Note that Dutch Faust is not wearing a House of David uniform, but one from his days with the Dallas Steers.

Three

1929–1934

The Golden Era

After the death of Benjamin Purnell, the colony split into two factions on February 25, 1929. One was led by Mary Purnell, and the other by Judge H.T. Dewhirst. Each faction fielded a team, and claimed to be the "true" House of David team. Francis Thorpe sided with Mary Purnell, and the famed Pepper Team went with Thorpe. From left to right, they are: Jesse Lee "Doc" Tally, George "Andy" Anderson, Francis Thorpe, and John Tucker.

The original colony separated into two colonies on March 14, 1930. The Dewhirst faction retained the House of David (HOD) name. Mary Purnell's colony assumed the name Israelite House of David as reorganized by Mary Purnell. Mary's colony also went by the name of City of David (COD). Both teams used the House of David name in promotions and newspaper articles. Pictured here is Judge H.T. Dewhirst.

Percy Walker left for Hot Springs, Arkansas, on March 27, 1930, with 14 men from the House of David. This contingency included third baseman, Dave "Eggs" Harrison, shortstop, Walter "Dutch" Faust, and Bob and Tom Dewhirst. Pictured here, from left to right, are: (front row) Dave "Eggs" Harrison, Percy Walker, Tom Dewhirst; (back row) Walter "Dutch" Faust and Hans "Barney" Dalager.

Featuring a picture of the 1928 House of David Traveling Team, this broadside was used to advertise both the House of David ball club, and later the City of David team. After the split in the colony, "Thorpe's" was added in ink to the poster to denote the City of David. Also pictured are Doc Tally (right) and John Tucker (bottom) along with Francis Thorpe (left). All were City of David members.

The City of David played in the very first night baseball game on April 17, 1930. Playing in Independence, Kansas, at Riverside Park, the City of David played against the Independence Producers before 1,200 fans. An *Independence Daily Reporter* article read: "First professional baseball by electric light. Independence witnesses world debut of night baseball on park of locals." The Producers defeated the City of David by a score of 9–1.

"In this bus we have traveled 75,000 miles. To the Pacific Coast three times, Atlantic Coast, and from Texas to Canada. Takening (sic) in forty states, and towns, playing 475 baseball games. Now a relic." Pictured here is Francis Thorpe, with the bus that he describes on the back of this photograph.

Ray Doan, promoter for the House of David, started sending three teams on the road during May 1931. These teams are the Eastern Traveling, Central States Traveling, and the Western Traveling teams. All used the House of David moniker. Pictured here are the Central States Traveling Team. From left to right, they are: John ?, Earl Boyersmith, Sidney Smith, Jack Crow, J.B. Boone, Oscar Wade, Jack Harron, Tom Dewhirst, Bob Dewhirst, Frank Wyland, Ernie Selby, Leo "Lefty" Wiltbank, Miller Wilson, Hobson "Hobie" Nelson, and Clay "Mud" Williams.

The 1931 City of David team while in Centralia, Washington. This photograph shows Dutch Witte before he became the City of David's promoter. Pictured here, from left to right: (seated) ? Drager, ? Bowers, ? Hoger, Joby Couch, Jesse Lee "Doc" Tally, George "Andy" Anderson, and ? Swift; (standing) Fred Radloff, ? Dunden, George "Lefty" Gilbert, John Tucker, Page Neve, Harold "Dutch" Witte, Thomas "Mac" McCafferty, and Herman "Flip" Fleming.

On September 22, 1931, The House of David, led by pitcher/manager Grover Cleveland Alexander lost to the St. Louis Cardinals by a score of 17–6, in the first-ever night game in Sportsman's Park. By utilizing the portable lighting system, the House of David was able to draw over nine thousand fans for the night exhibition. In contrast to the game played that afternoon, the Cardinals played the Reds drawing only 450 fans.

When Grover Cleveland Alexander was hired by Ray Doan in 1931 to manage one of the House of David teams, he was not required to grow a beard or pitch more than an inning or two. One of the things he had not counted on was "Donkey Ball." By the look on his face, one can only assume that he must be thinking, "I don't believe this was in my contract!"

The House of David and the City of David barnstormed the Kansas City Monarchs many times during the Depression. John Tucker related one story about batting against Satchel Paige. "Paige pitched a curve ball, and I hit it over the left field fence, 400 feet away. Satchel was as surprised as me, and he ran the bases with me and said 'Of all the people to hit a home run off 'Ole Satch' it had to be Tucker!' "

The Denver Post Tournament began in Denver on July 13, 1932 with the City of David team making their first appearance, and they eventually took third place. Playing against teams from Louisville, Colorado, Holdenville, Oklahoma, and Sioux City, Iowa, City of David players Red Lawrence and Lefty Gilbert both achieved batting averages of .600 during the tournament. The *Denver Post* reported: "At least 3,000 fans were unable to gain admittance to the Post Tournament as the greatest crowd in the history of the park battle to get in." Pictured, from left to right, are: (seated) Ray "Skeeter" Powell, John Tucker, George Anderson, Tessie (tournament assigned mascot), Francis Thorpe, Jesse Lee "Doc" Tally, William "Red" Lawrence, and "Pee Wee" Bass; (standing) Emery Savage, Herman "Flip" Fleming, Rolla "Softball" Mapel, Dick Atwell, Tom "Mac" McCafferty, Page Neve, George "Lefty" Gilbert, and Charles "Chuck" Noel.

The 1932 City of David team is pictured on the bench at the Denver Post Tournament. Even though the City of David team was heavily favored to win the tournament, they finished with a disappointing third place. They were also popular with the fans, as this photograph shows.

It's a hard life these touring ball players had. Once, coming from Saskatchewan, they ran into a rainstorm on the road and hit a stretch that was almost impassable. One of their cars bogged down, and it took the combined effort of most of the team to move it 9 miles in an hour and a half, and still they played a ball game. It makes this flat tire seem like a "broom handle!"

"This season's first and only night baseball game will be played this evening under lights at the House of David park in Benton Harbor between the colony's traveling teams of the central and eastern states. The game will be illuminated by an arc lighting system valued at $30,000." (Promotion for the 1933 season).

Rivaling the unusual attraction of the team itself was the giant portable lighting system carried for night games. The huge electric floodlights were mounted on telescoping poles on a fleet of trucks. The projectors were also mounted on 50-foot poles and placed around the playing field. A large truck carried the power plant and it was equipped with a 100,000-watt generator, powered by a 250-horsepower gasoline marine engine.

The House of David Baseball Team is pictured in Gary in 1933. Tom Dewhirst is seen here receiving one of the first aluminum bats made, from members of the Aluminum Corporation of America (ALCOA). It was not a "solid silver" bat, as some people have speculated, nor did Babe Ruth ever play with the team! He was offered the opportunity to participate, but his

contract was returned without being signed. He was pictured pulling the beard of a House of David player, but the photo was taken in Florida, where Louis Murphy's team conducted spring training. These are just two of the "myths" that have evolved over time concerning the House of David baseball team.

Due to an agreement made on April 27, 1933, with promoter Ray Doan, Francis Thorpe of the City of David did not send a team on the road for the 1933 season. Tally, Tucker, and Anderson all signed with Doan for the season. Tucker and Tally were assigned to the Western Traveling Team, which was managed by Grover Cleveland Alexander. George Anderson was assigned to the Eastern Travelers, which featured female pitcher Jackie Mitchell. Pictured here is the 1933 Western Travelers.

Grover Cleveland Alexander and Dick Atwell. Dick may have just told Alex about the time in Grand Junction, Colorado, when he was on third and Tucker broke for second. When the catcher's throw to second sailed into the outfield, Atwell scampered home, only to be tagged out. The "ball" that was pegged into the outfield turned out to be a potato. The call stood. Ole Pete looks a little bewildered by it all.

House of David Star First Sacker

BASEBALL
HOUSE OF DAVID

BILL HARDIN
Star Pitcher

FEATURING **CHIEF BENDER - - Philadelphia Athletics Pitching Star**
and WORLD'S SERIES HERO Will Start the Game

VS.

NIGHT BASEBALL
Played Under Our Own
$40,000
Lighting Plant!

CHIEF BENDER
Philadelphia Athletics Pitching Star

The Famous "Pepper Players"

See the Famous "Pepper" Game! - - - Worth the Price of Admission Alone!

The House of David has One of the Greatest Clubs to Ever Tour the Country! Many of the Players Have Turned Down Major League Offers!

GATES OPEN ONE HOUR EARLIER THAN USUAL! Game Will Be Played Rain or Shine!

VISIT House of David Park at Benton Harbor, Michigan! - - SEE House of David Exhibit at Chicago World's Fair!

On June 13, 1933, promoter Ray Doan signed former major league pitcher Charles "Chief" Bender. Bender was assigned to the Eastern Traveling Team as manager and star attraction. He played only part of the season, never again played for Ray Doan or the House of David.

"Alex had a car. His wife drove it. Sometimes he couldn't get to the games because he was too drunk. Sometimes he was so lit up you couldn't get him out of the dugout. He was a nice guy, but we couldn't depend on him. He only had to pitch one inning and when he couldn't do that, we had to let him go." (A quote from Eddie Deal about Grover Cleveland Alexander).

This photograph was taken in Santa Cruz, California, September 10, 1933. Bearded baseball players from the House of David at Benton Harbor, Michigan, defeated an All Star team from the California State League 4 to 2 here. Tucker was 4 for 5 at the plate for the House of David, while Alexander pitched two innings for the Davids and allowed no hits. He was relieved by Ambrose, who was in turn replaced by Tally.

Baseball tourists—and how! At least one game a day and sometimes a 400-mile drive during the night was the House of David program. Two weeks prior they had left Denver. Wednesday they won twice in Regina. Thursday they were in Estevan; Friday, Moose Jaw; Saturday, Saskatoon; Sunday, Salvador; and Monday, Edmonton. As one of the bearded boys said, "We don't even get time to send a postcard home."

On September 12, 1933, the Eastern Traveling Team played the St. Louis Cardinals at Sportsman Park. The House of David was victorious by a score of 8–6. George Anderson, a personal catcher for Jackie Mitchell in many games the Eastern team played, remembers this particular encounter as one of the highlights of his career. "They thought they were going to beat us, but we won. I got 2 for 4!"

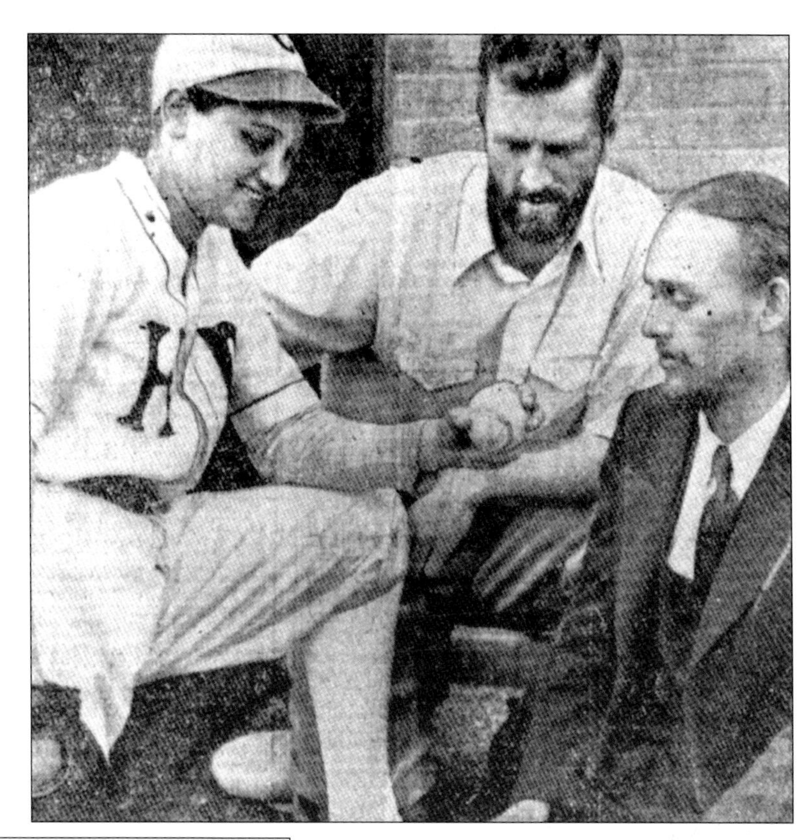

JUST AS GRACEFUL AS PITCHER

With the same easy motion that characterizes her in every athletic endeavor, Babe Didrikson throws a baseball. The wonder girl athlete from Texas will take the mound against St. Paul for the House of David nine Monday night at Lexington park.

Ray Doan signs Olympic Champion Mildred "Babe" Didrikson on April 17, 1934, to pitch for the House of David Western Traveling Team. Didrikson was paid $1,000 a month for her services. Grover Cleveland Alexander continued to be Eastern Traveling Team manager. Here Babe is pictured in an article depicting a game she played while with the House of David.

On April 29, 1934, Francis Thorpe sent out the City of David team after a one-year absence, and after not being paid by Ray Doan the full amount promised to him for not sending out a team. The House of David and Ray Doan continued to send three teams on the road.

Scribes who tabbed the House of David Nine a "traveling baseball team" spoke one great big mouthful. Their weekend itinerary was: Saturday night in Waco, Sunday afternoon in Austin, immediately after Sunday's game they departed for El Campo some 125 miles away, and played there Monday afternoon. They then returned to Austin and played again Monday night. All this, and 104 degrees in the shade!

Judge Harry Dewhirst filed a lawsuit against former House of David promoter Louis Murphy on May 23, 1934. For years, Murphy had been sending out touring teams from his Spring Valley, Illinois, headquarters, all of which were using the House of David name. Murphy's defense was that the House of David paid players and did not use colony members for their teams, and therefore the House of David name was public domain. The court ruled in favor of the House of David, stating that any team can field a team of bearded players, but the House of David name is the sole property of the colony. Louis Murphy would continue to send out barnstorming "House of David" teams until the early 1950s.

The 1934 Denver Post Tournament began on August 1, 1934. The House of David Eastern Traveling Team with Grover Cleveland Alexander took first place in the annual tournament, defeating the Kansas City Monarchs 2–0. Satchel Paige, on loan to promoter Ray Doan, pitched in the tournament, but was held back because Manager Alexander wanted him fresh for a second game, if it was needed. Paige was voted most popular player by winning three games in five days (a tournament record), striking out 44 batters in 28 innings, and hurling 23 consecutive scoreless frames. Other notables for the team were Art Murphy, who batted .455 in the tournament, and Lefty Tolles who achieved a .385 average during the course of the tournament. Pictured here, from left to right, are: (seated) Warren "Lefty" Weirman, Billy Joseph, Moon Mullen, Albert "Lefty" Tolles, Mel Ingram, Buster Blakeney, and Dewey Hill; (standing) John Cross, Spike Hunter, Art Murphy, Grover Cleveland Alexander, Lloyd Miller, Elmore E. Ambrose, and Carl Holland.

"Look out Kansas City Monarchs. That Satchel Paige has his car ready to take you for a ride. Paige, the greatest Negro pitcher in baseball, will pitch for the House of David in their post tournament game against the Monarchs, Negro champions of the world." The picture on the right shows Satchel talking over how he'll pitch the batters with Grover Cleveland, famous big league pitcher of another day and now managing the Bearded Beauties.

HOUSE OF DAVID 1938

Teams of bearded players suddenly sprang up all over America, and not to be outdone by their white brothers, a Colored House of David team was formed. Its date of origin is uncertain; it was around in the mid-1930s, although its existence was relatively short. Perhaps their lack of facial hair had something to do with their lack of success as an imitator of the Benton Harbor bunch.

On August 2, 1934, John Tucker was named Manager of the City of David team. Francis Thorpe returned to the City of David colony to assume a larger role in administrative responsibilities. Because of this change, Doc Tally was assigned the responsibility of part-time pitcher, and full-time Team Secretary.

In 1934, the City of David baseball team arrived in Mexico on September 7, and didn't return to the States for a month. A tough "local" team from Mexico City played against them for 11 of their 24 games. The City of David split the series with the talented team from south of the border—5 wins, 5 loses, and 1 tie. Pictured here is the City of David team in Mexico City.

The finish of a fast double play, Atwell to Hansen to Tucker, is captured in this photo. This was a familiar sight for those who were fortunate to see the 1934 City of David team play. It has been reported that during the 1934 season, this trio turned over three hundred double plays. One sportswriter said of the double play combination of Atwell, Hansen, and Tucker that they worked out like Tinker, Evers, and Chance used to in the big leagues.

"We have a two-ton chassis, wheel base around 180 inches. I think a ton and a half chassis would be plenty large for you. The reason I chose a two-ton job, was the air-booster brakes for the mountains. Our gas average for the season was about twelve (12) miles per gallon, and changed oil every thousand miles without adding any. Your Dodge dealer will be glad to give you all the details." (John Tucker.)

A major attraction for all House of David teams was the Pepper Game. The Pepper Game originated around 1922, when Doc Tally and Dutch Faust started playing a game called "High/Low" between innings of games when the House of David Band played. The game evolved into the Pepper Game around 1926, when John Tucker joined the group. When Dutch Faust left to play minor league baseball, George Anderson joined the exhibition. When the colony divided, each group kept a Pepper Team. Even imitators utilized the spectacle.

The Pepper Game was usually performed in the middle of the fifth inning, with the three performers lined up approximately 2 feet apart. A fourth player acted as a batter and hit to the group. Each player had a repertoire of moves they performed. Perhaps a behind-the-back toss, a fake throw to one of the others, or a roll of the ball down their arms.

Four

PLAYER BIOS

GEORGE "ANDY" ANDERSON: Catcher/Third Base/Utility for House of David, 1927–1929, for City of David, 1930–1955, Manager, 1946–1955. George "Andy" Anderson came to the House of David Colony from Australia in 1920. He began playing baseball at ten years old and soon joined the House of David Junior team. At age 13, he moved up to the Home team, and in mid-July of 1927, at age 17, he joined the celebrated Traveling Team in Minneapolis, Minnesota. He remained an integral part of House of David/City of David baseball for almost four decades.

George broke in as a catcher, but it wasn't long before he was utilized at second, short, and third. He remained at the "hot corner" until the late 1940s, when he moved across the diamond to play first. He played every position on the field before his noteworthy career came to a close in 1956. George was asked, "so you were 45 when you stopped playing ball?" He replied, "About that." "Were you still playing good?" To which he replied, "Oh Yeah!"

"We played a lot of hit and run, bunt the runner over. We were fundamentally sound." And fundamentally sound is what George was. For seven years in the 1930s, George had 1,231 hits in 3,694 at bats. That is a composite average of .333. His best year was 1937 when he had 284 hits, and a batting average of .362.

The House of David/City of David barnstormed for a number of years with the Kansas City Monarchs, Satchel Paige's All Stars, and later the Harlem Globetrotters.

On Satch, George had this to say: "He was one of the greatest pitchers there ever was...but I got lots of hits off him. I wasn't a big swing hitter, I was left handed and I'd just punch his fast ball over shortstop."

MONROE WULFF: Utility for House of David, 1915–1925. Known for his fence-rattling doubles, Monroe had a long career with the team. His ability to hit the ball hard made him a potential starter; however, his strikeouts kept him from joining the Traveling Team on a permanent basis. His most productive year was in 1925, when he hit for a .260 batting average. Monroe continued as a colony member for the City of David, where he lived until his death in 1936.

JESSE LEE "DOC" TALLY: Outfield/Pitcher for House of David, 1915–1929, City of David 1930–1950. Jesse Lee "Doc" Tally arrived at the House of David from Mississippi on October 25, 1914, when he was 18 years old. Arriving with him were his father and three brothers. The next spring, Doc and brother, Swaney, were instrumental in helping to start the baseball team.

A knuckleball pitcher, Doc pitched the team to a county championship in the first year of the team's existence. As much as he was a good right-handed pitcher, Doc was also an excellent left-handed hitting outfielder. Known for his power as well as his ability to hit for average, bunt, or sacrifice, Doc would do anything to help the team generate a run.

In 1925, he batted .303, and the 1926 season showed his average to be .301, with five homeruns. Around this time, Doc, along with colony member Dutch Faust, created the famed Pepper Game. Later John Tucker joined the Pepper Team, and George Anderson replaced Faust, to create one of the most famous exhibitions in barnstorming baseball.

By the 1934 season, new manager John Tucker turned the 38-year-old Tally into a part-time pitcher, as well as Team Secretary/Treasurer. He helped with the younger players, and it was said he kept an "eagle eye" on the gate money. During the war years, the team was placed on hiatus, and Doc, at the request of friend John Tucker, pitched occasionally for the Auto Specialties Team of St. Joseph. After the war was over, Doc and George Anderson reformed the team with Doc retaining his Secretary/Treasurer responsibilities full-time. In a 1948 interview, Tally estimated that he appeared in more than 2,200 games as an outfielder and pitcher.

On the morning of January 25, 1950, while preparing for his 36th season, Doc died suddenly. No explanation was ever given. He was 53 years old.

FRANCIS THORPE: House of David Manager, 1912–1929, City of David Manager, 1930–1934. Francis arrived at the House of David on December 7, 1904, when he was 28 years old, and was made Colony Secretary within four years. Being a sport enthusiast, he created the baseball team in 1914. Francis was very instrumental in the development and nurturing of team members through most of the 1920s. Replaced by Judge H.T. Dewhirst as Colony Secretary in 1921, Francis remained a pillar of the organization.

The colony eventually divided, and Mary Purnell and her new City of David colony moved into quarters across the street from the original colony. Francis assumed the responsibility of Colony Secretary, Business Manager, and Colony Trustee. He continued to manage the baseball team. In 1934, at the request of Mary Purnell, he turned the team over to John Tucker, and assumed more day-to-day responsibilities.

Francis remained a trustee and financial manager of the colony until his death on September 9, 1957, from gall bladder ailments related to diabetes. He was 81 at the time of his death.

PAUL MOONEY: Pitcher for House of David, 1914–1926. One of the original members of the House of David when his family joined in 1905, Paul was also on the first House of David baseball team. By 1917, Paul was the team's premiere pitcher, compiling a 10–8 record. He appeared in 20 games, started 18, and completed 17 of his starts. It was a no-hitter on October 5, 1919, that started a long stream of offers from professional clubs. It was reported that he once received a $20,000 offer from the Chicago Cubs, but refused due to the requirement that he cut his hair. Evidence of his notoriety can be validated by this poem that appeared in *The Sporting News* on December 11, 1919.

When the pitcher Mooney mounts the hill
With hair and whiskers flowing,
The stuff he'll put upon the pill
Will have the batters going.

They will not even make a foul
Or hammer out a fair ball;
And they will make an awful howl
When Mooney hurls the hair ball.

Paul Mooney continued his extraordinary pitching until an arm injury ended his career in the mid-1920s.

HANS "BARNEY" DALAGER: Driver/Baggage Man for House of David, 1919–1936. Born in Minnesota on August 19, 1884, he arrived at the House of David colony via Canada, on September 20, 1918. He quickly assumed a role with the baseball team as a driver for one of the autos, and worked closely with Bill Frye as a baggage man and gate man. He was given the nickname of "Barney" for his driving prowess, after famous Indianapolis racer Barney Oldfield. It was said that Dalager would oftentimes be the last to leave, and the first to show up at the next destination. He worked for the team until they purchased a bus in the mid-1930s, and he then drove a truck for the colony. His son Lloyd made them the first and only father and son combination on the colony team. He stayed with the House of David colony right up to his death in 1972 at age 87.

PERCY WALKER: Pitcher for House of David, 1920–1930, Manager, 1929–1930. Born on December 17, 1893, Percy Walker came to the House of David colony around 1918 from his home in Pennsylvania. By 1920, he was playing for the home team, mostly as a pitcher. Between 1922 and 1928 he played off and on, always on the home team. During the spring of 1928, he was selected to be the manager of the Dewhirst Faction House of David team. He accepted the role and occasionally had to compete for players with Francis Thorpe, manager of the Mary Purnell Faction. Percy still started himself as a pitcher, but eventually turned over management of the team to the Dewhirst brothers, in particular Tom Dewhirst. He lived the rest of his life working at the House of David colony until his death in October of 1953.

DWIGHT "Zeke" BAUSCHKE: Second Base/Shortstop for House of David, 1921–1926. Zeke and his family were original members of the House of David, and helped create the colony by donating the land that the colony now sits on. He was also a member of the House of David traveling band, and participated on band tours when he was not playing baseball. "Sometimes when we would go out east and play in the big cities, and the band would be booked there at the same time, we'd have to go out and hire some local fellows to play on the ball team 'cause half of the ball club would leave to go play with the band" (Zeke Bauschke interview, 1998.) Zeke played baseball from 1921 to 1926 before leaving the colony to move to Detroit to become a professional musician. He eventually settled in Inverness, Florida, where he died in 1998.

WALTER "DUTCH" FAUST: Shortstop/Second Base for House of David, 1920–1926, 1929 City of David (Hired Player), 1930–1931, House of David (Hired Player), 1933–1935. Dutch lived at the House of David lumber operation on High Island, where he was noticed for his multiple athletic abilities. He started playing for the home team around 1920, and started hitting the road with the team around 1922. Dutch, along with Doc Tally, were the originators of the famed House of David Pepper Team. On March 4, 1926, Dutch signed a contract to play for the Dallas Steers of the Texas Association. Playing one year in Texas, then the following year in Ohio, Dutch returned to the colony after a series of injuries. Returning home, Dutch played for the colony as a hired player. Playing with both the City of David and House of David until about 1935, Dutch then left, never to return. His whereabouts were never established, and rumors abound as to how he ended up.

JOHN "LONG JOHN" TUCKER: First Base for House of David, 1923–1929, City of David, 1930–1942, Manager 1934-1942. Born in Tyler, Texas, in 1902, John and his family arrived at the House of David in 1915. Assigned to High Island, the colony lumber operation, John was quickly noticed for his athletic abilities. Although he was eventually summoned back to the colony in 1919 to start on the Junior Team, the rest of the Tucker family remained on High Island for another seven years. By 1923, John was assigned to the Home Team, and by 1925, he was the backup first baseman for the Traveling Team. In his first year, John participated in 89 games and had a batting average of .279. By the time the 1926 season came around, John found himself the starting first baseman for the team.

His enthusiasm was the trait that got John into the Pepper Game with George Anderson and Doc Tally. John was also known to catch baseballs between his legs and behind his back while playing first base.

After the colony divided, John played for the City of David team and took over as manager in 1934. In 1942, John decided to leave the colony to take a job with the Auto Specialties team of St. Joseph. His last year as a player was in 1947, but he coached until the company stopped fielding a team in 1957. After retiring, he lived to the ripe old age of 89, when in March of 1991, he died of natural causes.

John Tucker spent his entire adult life involved in baseball. He subscribed to four rules that he felt made a good ball player great:

1. "You can't take your work home with you."
2. "Go to bed the same day you get up."
3. "Never go on a liquid diet." (Inferring alcohol.)
4. "Last, but not least, you got to be able to hit that curveball."

DAVE "EGGS" HARRISON: Third Base for House of David, 1927–1936. Nearly a lifetime member of the House of David, Harrison was born April 19, 1904, in Australia, and arrived in Benton Harbor in 1905. His first experience with the baseball team was as the original batboy. From that experience, Dave was able to earn a spot on the home team by 1921, and by 1925 was the Traveling Team's third baseman.

A good hitter and base stealer, he obtained a .314 batting average in 1926, his first complete season traveling. In 1932, he was picked to play on the Traveling Team that was to be managed by Grover Cleveland Alexander, and rewarded the team with a .354 batting average. In addition, during that year, he was offered multiple tryouts with professional teams, and became the middle member of the House of David Pepper Team.

Ending his career around 1936 after playing close to 15 years, he was content to live out his time working around the colony grounds, where he died the morning of Christmas Eve 1982, at the age of 78.

HAROLD "PUP' SMITH: Pitcher for House of David, 1925. Harold E. "Pup" Smith, born October 14, 1905, (far left) joined the Traveling Team in 1925. Used primarily as a pitcher, he was one of the few non-colony members recruited by the House of David in the mid-twenties. His best performance came on August 19th, when he hurled a three-hit shutout over Worthington, Minnesota.

FRANK WYLAND: Outfield for House of David, 1915–1931. Wyland, who was the House of David security force (he was deputized by the sheriff's office), did not play as a full-time endeavor. He started with the team as a pitcher, but once the team became better, he moved his strength to the outfield. Never playing on the Traveling Team, Wyland felt his other responsibilities were more important. Also a boxer, he was used as an attraction at the House of David Park for sparring sessions.

LLOYD "BARNEY" DALAGER: Catcher/Utility for House of David, 1927–1936, 1942–1947. Born September 14, 1913, in Saskatchewan, Canada, Lloyd was a member of the Junior team in 1927, and was around baseball for most of his young life. His father, Barney Dalager, was with the House of David teams for 18 years. In 1936, Lloyd played for the Central States traveling team, as a backup catcher behind Eddie Deal and in right field. He was a line drive-type hitter, who was to be counted on in the clutch. He was regarded by Tom Dewhirst as a "real comer." Lloyd was also a member of the House of David version of the Pepper Game, along with Deal and Dave Harrison. When the House of David quit sending out a Traveling Team in 1937, Lloyd took up softball. He played locally for both the Portsmouth Ales and Kamm's Beer. His usual position on these teams was behind the plate.

George Anderson once asked Lloyd (bottom row, far right) during this time if he would like to go on the road with him. Regretfully, colony duties kept Lloyd at home. When the House of David fielded a team again and began playing on weekends, Lloyd returned to baseball. His career came to an end when he tore cartilage in his right knee. Lloyd is still an active member of the colony, and currently holds the position of President of the House of David.

ALBERT "LEFTY" TOLLES: Outfield/Pitcher for House of David, 1929–1935. Originally from South Haven, Michigan, Lefty was a star for the Michigan State baseball team before being recruited by the colony. Lefty played in the field when he was not on the mound and batted .385 in the 1934 Denver Post Tournament, helping the team win the championship. Lefty also played in the 1936 Denver Post Tournament after being recruited by Louis Murphy to participate on his team.

BILL HECKMAN: Pitcher/First Base/Outfield for House of David, 1925–1935, First Base for City of David, 1930. Bill Heckman was one of the first non-colony players to be hired by the House of David, beginning his tenure with the club as early as 1924. He used to travel from Detroit to Benton Harbor to pitch on Sundays, and it wasn't long before he was offered a full- time position on the team. He began his career with the Davids as a pitcher, but because of his ability to hit for power, he was soon playing outfield when he wasn't on the mound. After his single season with the City of David, he rejoined the House of David team, where he held down the first base position for a number of years. Bill was also quite a ladies' man. According to Eddie Deal, "All the girls on the circuit knew our first basemen Bill Heckman. When we'd pull into town they'd yell out, 'Where's Willie?' He'd yell back 'Here I am Baby!' and we wouldn't see him until the game started."

BOB DEWHIRST: Pitcher/First Base for House of David, 1928–1936. Bob came with his family to the colony in 1920 from California. Like his brother Tom, he assimilated quickly into the colony life, and baseball was just one of the endeavors Bob pursued. Not exactly a part-time player, Bob played primarily on the various home teams. He was known as a good pitcher and a decent hitter. When other teams were on the road, Bob would fill in as the Home Team Manager. Although he played baseball, his primary function was to play in the band. He led the House of David Traveling Orchestra and was a composer. After his playing days, Bob was given the responsibility of running the House of David fruit farm operations. He was also the Colony Secretary up until his death in 1966.

H. TOM DEWHIRST: Outfield for House of David, 1928–1937, Manager, 1931–1937. Tom Dewhirst arrived in Benton Harbor with his parents and brother in 1920, from California, when he was just 11 years old. As with all players, he started on the Junior Team, and in 1928, at the age of 19, Tom had made the home team and was named manager of the Central States Traveling Team by 1931. At 6' 2" and 220 pounds, Tom was an imposing figure at the plate, and earned a reputation as a devastating power hitter. From 1929 to 1933, Tom was one of the team's leaders in home runs, with a seasonal average of 38. A good business person, Tom was adamant that his teams never run up the scores on less talented opponents. His motive for this excellent sportsmanship was that he wanted to make sure his team was invited back.

Tom used this common sense approach to other endeavors after his playing days were over, when he was assigned to take over the House of David agriculture operations and the House of David Cold Storage Facility. During his career in the produce industry, Tom was the President of the Twin Cities Area Chamber of Commerce, the 1960 Agriculture's Man of the Year, and a member of the Benton Harbor Market Board.

After the House of David retired their agricultural operations, Tom became Colony Secretary in 1966, and lived out his life giving riotous lectures to schoolchildren and acting as the House of David Team historian. A gracious host, Tom was eager and ready to reminisce about his playing days with all visitors until his death in 1996 at age 87.

EDDIE DEAL: Catcher for House of David, 1929–1942, Manager, 1936–1942. Edward F. Deal was born September 10, 1901. He was often called "The Real Deal," "The New Deal," and sometimes just "The Clown." Eddie joined the House of David baseball team in 1929. He continued with the club until 1942—the longest tenure of any non-colony member.

When the Colony split in 1930, Eddie became a mainstay behind the plate for the House of David Central States traveling team until 1936. At that time, in addition to his job behind the plate, he took on the managerial duties of the House of David "home" team. He was also a primary player in the local version of the Pepper Game, as well as a fan favorite.

He caught both Alexander and Babe Didrikson while with the House of David. "I can remember sometimes just sitting on the bench and I'd say to myself, 'This is great!' They're paying me to do something I love to do."

Eddie was once asked if the secret of his longevity could be described as no smoking, no drinking, no meat, no sex. His reply was, "You could say that. I just believe in smiling and being happy." Eddie "The New Deal" will be 99 in September, 2000.

"In critical situations, I liked to tell the batters what was coming. 'Tell you what I'm going to do, a fastball, chest high, right down the middle. I want to see you get a base hit.' The batter would back out and say catchers are all damn liars. I'd say 'You couldn't hit a fly in the ass with a screen door.' The pitch would be a fastball right down the middle and they'd never expect it."

HERMAN "FLIP" FLEMING: Catcher for City of David, 1929–1935, House of David, 1933. Fleming was born May 7, 1898, and came to the team in 1929, after being a product of the Boston Braves organization. Playing from 1929 to 1935, Flip was the every-day catcher for the City of David, and was known to be an excellent athlete who possessed all of the physical and mental necessities to play the position. More than once in old team box scores, it was noted that Fleming played the game the way it was supposed to be—with hustle. Not known as a powerful hitter, he could get on base when needed and move a runner over when it was necessary. He managed to obtain a .375 batting average during the 1932 Denver Post Tournament. When the City of David did not field a team for 1933, Flip moved over to the House of David Eastern Traveling Team for the season. It is said he would wax on about his great days with the team up until his death in 1965.

GROVER CLEVELAND ALEXANDER: Pitcher/Manager for House of David, 1931–1935. Born in Elba, Nebraska, in 1887, Grover Cleveland Alexander started his career in 1911 with the Philadelphia Phillies, and won 28 games in that rookie season, a league record. He continued playing until 1930, while compiling a 373–208 win-loss record with the Phillies, Chicago Cubs, and St. Louis Cardinals.

In 1931, he was persuaded by promoter Ray Doan to join the House of David Team. His role was defined as manager, pitcher, and box office drawing card. The only player not required to grow a beard, he was given an additional 35¢ a day for razor money, which was used primarily to purchase alcohol. His drinking problem kept Alexander from being the leader that Doan wanted him to be. Alexander's biggest year with the House of David was the 1934 season when Satchel Paige was recruited to play for the team in the Denver Post Tournament, which they won.

Grover Cleveland Alexander ended his relationship with Ray Doan and the House of David Baseball Team after the 1935 season, and described his adventures in a less than a favorable manner. He was quoted as saying, "I was advertised like the elephant in the circus and had to pitch an inning or so every game. I always picked the eighth or ninth inning and prayed for rain."

With his baseball career officially over, Alexander moved from a local radio job to a series of odd jobs, most being lost due to his heavy drinking. At that point in his life he became estranged from most of the people closest to him. He then was inducted into the Baseball Hall of Fame in 1938, as one of the first 13 members in that introductory year. He eventually died of a suspected heart attack on November 4, 1950. He was 63 years old.

Opposite: **RICHARD "DICK" ATWELL:** Shortstop for City of David, 1932, House of David, 1933, City of David, 1934–1937. Richard "Dick" Atwell was born January 31, 1910. He began playing minor league ball in 1929, right out of high school. He was with the Western League two years and Mississippi Valley one year, before joining the City of David in 1932. He continued his association with the City of David/House of David for the next five years, leaving briefly in 1934 for a tryout with the San Francisco Seals (Joe DiMaggio's minor league team), and again in 1937 for a spot on the Los Angles Angels.

A fine fielding shortstop, Dick could also hit for power, averaging over 20 home runs per season. In 1934, according to a letter from John Tucker, the City of David manager, he hit over 40 home runs, and was offered a $2 bonus for every circuit clout he hit in 1935.

Dick left baseball to join the Pasadena Fire Department in 1938, where he remained until 1970, when he retired after 32 years of service. He passed away on February 11, 1985.

Dick Atwell was a favorite of fans and management alike, as is evidenced in this letter from 1936. "We have all the other boys signed up, with two or three new men at a much reduced salary and some of the others a salary cut. I guess we can afford to pay you the $190 per month. You will be the highest paid man on the club. Your conduct is worth something to us."

HOLMAN "PEE WEE" BASS: Pitcher for City of David, 1930–1939. Bass (left) a diminutive southpaw sensation for the City of David, began his tenth season on the team in 1939. He led the team in 1935 with 34 wins and 9 losses. He had a steak of 24 consecutive victories. He also hurled two no-hit ball games while with Corpus Christi of the Texas League.

GERMAIN "GERRY" BUSH: Catcher for House of David, 1932–1935. Born in Watertown, New York, on February 15, 1905, Germain "Gerry" Bush originally came to the House of David to work in their machine shop. Once they learned of his past, formerly being a catcher in Erie, Pennsylvania, he was given the responsibility of backing up catcher Eddie Deal, and driving the team bus.

From 1932 to 1935, Gerry spent his time tolling in all of his responsibilities, and loved every minute of it. Though he did not play every day, he was said to have been extremely thrilled to be allowed to participate with the House of David Baseball team. Keeping it in the family, he eventually married House of David Girl's Team player Helen Godwin. He lived out his rewarding life in Rome, New York, until April 1, 1968.

VIRNE BEATRICE "JACKIE" MITCHELL: Pitcher for House of David, 1933. Mitchell came on to the scene as a 17-year-old pitching phenomenon for the Class AA Chattanooga Lookouts. Signed to the Lookouts, she participated in an exhibition game between the Lookouts and the New York Yankees, on April 2, 1931. She was sent in to relieve after only two batters. The first batter, Babe Ruth, was fanned in just four pitches. The next batter, Lou Gehrig, struck out swinging on only three pitches. Within a few days, Baseball Commissioner Landis voided Mitchell's contract because baseball was too rough of a sport for women.

In 1933, she was signed to pitch for the Eastern Traveling Team. Being used primarily as a drawing card, Jackie would pitch only in the beginning of the game. Because she was never in the game long enough to be considered the pitcher of record, she did not accumulate a won/loss record.

Jackie only played for the House of David during the 1933 season, but continued to participate in exhibitions for another half-dozen years, before she returned to Chattanooga. She died in 1987 when she was 73 years old.

JOHN "SLICK" CROSS: First Baseman for House of David, 1933–1934. John "Slick" Cross joined the House of David team May 10th, 1933, after a successful stint in the London-Michigan-Ontario League where he hit 32 triples in 1925—a minor league record. While with Louisville, it was written about John that "his follow-through was like Babe Ruth's." There were apparently some similarities. In his first season with the House of David, John swatted 43 home runs.

In 1934, he contributed to the House of David victory in the final game of the Denver Post Tournament with a double off the centerfield fence that scored what proved to be the winning run in a 2–0 victory over the Kansas City Monarchs. He went on to play for the Post Product of Battle Creek, and in 1937, was named to the second All Tournament team of the Amateur World Series.

ALVIN "AL" NUSSER: Pitcher for City of David, 1934, 1936. Alvin "Al" Nusser was born in Chicago on October 31, 1909. He joined the City of David ball club in 1934. After a year with the Portsmouth Pirates in '35, he rejoined the Davids for the '36 season. He also saw action with Kansas City of the American Association in '37, Spokane and Bellingham of the Western International League in '38, and was later signed by the Chicago Cubs of the National League. After a brief visit to "the show," he took over mound duties for the Wichita Water Company, a semi-pro ball club.

His best year with the City of David was in 1934, when he pitched in 65 games for 381 innings, winning 37 and losing 7. During these games, he struck out 361 batters and had an earned run average of 2.25. Al Nusser passed away on October 31, 1998.

MILDRED "BABE" DIDRIKSON: Pitcher for House of David, 1934. Born in Port Arthur, Texas, on June 26, 1914, Babe gravitated to sports at an early age. In 1930, she was hired by an insurance company because of her ability to type over 80 words a minute and average over 40 points a game in basketball. During this same time, Babe competed in many AAU track meets. The 1932 AAU Track and Field Nationals also doubled as an Olympic qualifying event. Earning the right to participate in the 1932 Olympics, she won gold medals for the javelin and hurdles, and silver for the high jump. Returning to Texas, she met promoter Ray Doan, who helped her form the Babe Didrikson All-American Basketball Team. During the spring of 1934, Babe toured baseball spring training camps, competing against Major League players. Seeing this, Doan hired her to travel with one of his House of David teams. Babe was assigned to the Western States Traveling Team, and was scheduled to only pitch the first two innings of every game. She made her House of David debut on May 7th, against Chicago's Logan Squares.

HOUSE OF DAVID

The House of David Pepper Game is one of the Greatest Baseball Juggling Acts Ever Known.

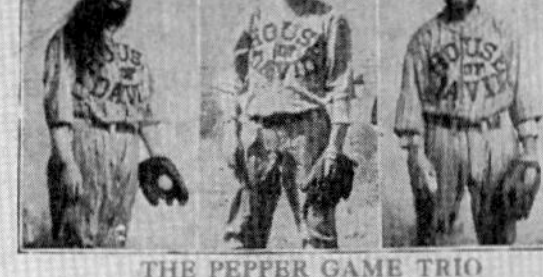
THE PEPPER GAME TRIO

Some of the Stars Developed by the House of David Baseball Club

BABE DIDRIKSON
World's Greatest Girl Athlete and baseball player

The 1934 Western Travelers finished their season with a game against Joe Green's Colored Chicago Giants. The House of David won the game 3–2 with Babe pitching only the first inning. She retired the side in order, and thus ended her baseball career. Being a natural golfer, Babe played in her first tournament in October 1934. Between 1944 and 1947, she won 22 amateur tournaments, and in 1947, she won the British Amateur Tournament. Following the 1947 season, she declared herself a professional and joined the Women's Professional Golf Association. During 1949, she helped form the Ladies Professional Golf Association (LPGA). She was named Female Athlete of the Year for 1947, 1950, and 1954, adding to her previously earned titles from 1932, 1945, and 1946. During the 1953 season, she was diagnosed with colon cancer and had to undergo emergency colostomy surgery. Four months later, she returned to the LPGA tour and was awarded the Ben Hogan Trophy for Comeback Player of the Year. She continued to compete until finally succumbing to the disease on September 27, 1956.

ROY HUTSON: Outfielder for City of David, 1933–1936. Born February 27, 1902, in Missouri, Hutson had a "cup of coffee" with the Brooklyn Dodgers in 1925, and played in the Texas League before coming to the City of David. His best year with them came in 1935, when he hit .370, and was known as a consistent player for the team. However, his life was short-lived, and he died on May 20, 1957, in La Mesa, California.

CLEO GLENN "LEFTY" DACUS: Pitcher for City of David, 1936. Born in 1907 in Arkansas, Dacus was a former player in the Cleveland Indians organization, who primarily played for the New Orleans Pelicans. In the first game he pitched for the City of David, Glen held the Kansas City Monarchs to a 3–1 decision. However, his career with the team was short-lived, and he left before the '36 season ended. He eventually settled in Madison County, Illinois, where he died in 1972.

CECIL TUCKER: Pitcher/First Base for City of David, 1935–1937. Cecil Tucker, born June 10, 1911, was the last rookie to come from within the colony. Younger brother of John Tucker, Cecil joined the City of David Traveling Team in the spring of 1935, after showing promise while playing ball locally. Used primarily as a spot starter, Cecil was still able to compile a 15–1 pitching record. When John went down with a fractured leg on August 24, Cecil was asked to fill in at first base for him—a position that was not unfamiliar to him. That winter, Cecil developed a lingering illness and was unable to travel with the team until fall when they journeyed to Hawaii. His playing time on this tour was limited, and his duties were mainly that of a scorekeeper. In early spring of 1937, while preparing for another season, Cecil died of cancer. He was 26 years old.

FRED "ZEKE" LARSON: Pitcher for City of David, 1936. Fred "Zeke" Larson was born November 14, 1902. He is pictured here with his battery mates from the 1936 City of David team. They are, from left to right: Fred Larson, Don Hendrickson, Al Nusser, and Cleo "Glenn" Dacus. Fred was pitching semi-pro ball for Charles City, Iowa, when they played the House of David team. "I guess Tucker liked what he saw and signed me. We signed no contract with the Davids, a handshake was binding. You could leave anytime you wanted, but I stayed the whole summer, in part because the pitchers were paid a bonus for every game they won." He played 91 games with the City of David that summer and, reluctantly, after a double-header in Chicago on September 1, returned to his job as a high school baseball coach. "A job nowhere near as much fun as his summer of beards and baseball had been." Fred "Zeke" Larson is currently enjoying his 98th season.

CLIFFORD "COUNT" CLAY: Pitcher for City of David, 1937–1941. 1941 was the Count's fifth season with the City of David. He was one of their ace pitchers, and because of his power at the plate, often filled in as a pinch hitter and an outfielder. He spent his spare time coaching and clowning at first and third base, where he had built up a large following all over the country.

WILLARD "BILL" PIKE: Outfield for City of David, 1938–1939. A former player in the Texas League, Pike came to the City of David because of his bat. Noted for his power hitting, he did not disappoint the team. In 1938 he hit 28 homeruns in the 173 game season.

LEW HUMMEL: Catcher for City of David, 1946–1947. Lew Hummel was a member of the City of David team in both 1946 and 1947. As a catcher, Lew appeared in almost every game. For most of the 1946 season, he batted in the cleanup spot, compiling a batting average of .335 and 15 home runs to his credit. Before the service, he had played class B ball in the Inter-state league and class A ball in the Eastern League.

DICK HUMMEL: Pitcher for City of David, 1946–1947. Dick Hummel joined his brother Lew on the 1946 City of David team in early June. He was one of the regular pitchers, starting 19 games, winning 12 and dropping 7. He appeared in many more games as a relief pitcher, and batted .285 for the season. Dick Hummel continued to be active in baseball for the next 30 years, playing, coaching, and umpiring, at both high school and college levels.

PAUL "PETE" JARVIS: Utility for City of David, 1946–1947. Paul "Pete" Jarvis was recruited by Lew Hummel and played with the City of David in both 1946 and 1947. In '46, he was used primarily at first base, shortstop, and third. The 1947 season saw him play every position but pitcher and catcher. When Lenny "Rocky" Kallis broke his leg, Paul was asked to fill in on the famed Pepper Game. It was a task he both enjoyed and executed well.

DICK WYKOFF: Pitcher for City of David, 1934–1948. A former player with Columbus of the American Association, Wykoff was one of the more familiar non-colony faces. A very durable and smart pitcher, he was also a timely hitter and won a number of his own ball games with his bat. When the City of David team reformed in 1946, Wykoff was called upon to once more don their uniform. He continued with the team through the 1948 season.

Five

1935–1939

The Journey Continues

The 1935 City of David Home Team is pictured above. Not having a home ballpark, this team played out by the Benton Harbor Airport. They are, from left to right: (kneeling) Uber Tucker, Amos Edwards, and Jimmy Crow; (standing) Henry Tart, Melvin Tucker, Louie Buck, Frank Kolesar, Cecil Tucker, Miles Crow, Ben Caudle, Everett Buck, and Bill Frye.

"Very few roads were marked west of the Mississippi. We traveled in three twelve-cylinder passenger Packard cars. Later we traveled in two Studebakers and a Packard, and at times, we traveled in a private bus. Quite frequently, while driving, we had to open up cattle fences, drive the cars through, get out, and close the gate before the cattle would get out. In those days, we carried four extra tires, and it was not until the late twenties that the first 50,000-mile guarantee tires came to the market. Many times, we would run into wet water where the clay would lock the tires to the drums, and we would have to stop the cars. We would fix up one tire at a time. This became quite a task, because you had to make sure we had a solid foundation for the jack or it would sink into the clay." (Interview with Tom Dewhirst, 1991.) Left to right are Tom Dewhirst, Hans "Barney" Dalager, and Percy Walker.

Grover Cleveland Alexander and Bob Dewhirst, photographed here on the colony grounds. Not as well known for his baseball abilities as his brother Tom, Bob was an accomplished musician. He played a number of different instruments, did arrangements, and even wrote a few songs of his own. Evidently, this was music to Alex's ears, as it is one of the few photos where we see him smiling.

COMING!! - Season's Greatest Attraction!

House of David Baseball Club

Direct from Benton Harbor, Michigan

America's Most Outstanding Traveling Team Now Playing Their 21st Season!

PRESS COMMENTS ON SOME OF LAST YEAR'S GAMES:

Spend Your 1935 Vacation at House of David Park, Benton Harbor, Michigan

MICHIGAN'S GREATEST SUMMER RESORT! IN THE HEART OF THE FRUIT BELT!

This was a 1935 press sheet released by the House of David to commemorate some of the Central States Traveling Team's accomplishments over the previous season. Featured in the photo portion is Eddie Deal. One of the quotes from Kewanee, Illinois claims "10,000 fans see long beards defeat Legion 8–0." That was more people than many major league parks were drawing at the time.

On March 25, 1935, the City of David players left Benton Harbor for spring training in Overton, Texas. They traveled over 600 miles the first day before stopping in Springfield, Missouri. They arrived in Overton the next night and began workouts at the Humble Ball Park the following morning. Their first game of the season was played on March 31, a 14–4 victory over the local Greenville club.

"Trouble with the law? Rarely! However, a $15 ticket for an improper taillight seems a bit excessive, even by today's standards! Perhaps it was issued in retaliation for the 18–11 drubbing the local boys received at the hands of the Israelite 9 that afternoon." (Entry in Cecil Tucker's diary, April 3, 1935, Mt. Pleasant, Texas.)

"House of David first baseman may have set record in game at Refugio, Texas." In a game against the Refugio Fireman, on April 20, 1935, which the City of David won 13–3, John Tucker made 23 of his teams 27 putouts during the nine innings. He made 14 putouts in a row, and in 6 of the 9 rounds, he was credited with every putout.

Donkey baseball was a gimmick used often by promoter Ray Doan. All players, except for pitcher and catcher were required to ride donkeys during the course of the game. They fielded the ball while on the donkey, or as far as the reins would allow them. Hitters batted in the normal manner, but once the ball was hit, they had to mount a donkey and navigate their way around the bases.

On June 4, 1935, the House of David, utilizing their portable lighting system, played the Newark Eagles in the very first night game held at Ebbets Field. The lighting system, rented from the Kansas City Monarchs, was used for only part of the season by one of the House of David Traveling Teams.

In a quote by Grover Cleveland Alexander, he explained, "If you want to see the world, join the Navy. If you want to see the United States, join the House of David Baseball team." A nomadic group of ball players, it was not unusual for the House of David and City of David teams to log more than 30,000 miles a year while criss-crossing the United States.

The 1935 House of David Central States Traveling Team is pictured in front of the Blatz Brewery. Though it was not allowed for colony members, the House of David was known to wager their opponents for kegs of beer. From the looks of this photograph, it appears that the House of David was victorious, and that the boys have come to collect their winnings.

As popular as the David's baseball team was, so, apparently, was their mode of transportation. Some local fans check out their bus in this photo. One afternoon, the team arrived in Hershel, Canada, which was really just a crossroads in the prairie with a couple of buildings. When the teams saw the deserted bleachers, they got ready to pack it up. The Canadian promoter insisted they stay and play. Before the day was over, 1,500 enthusiastic fans had turned out.

The House of David Central States Travelers are pictured during the mid-1930s, while in Wisconsin. This team played primarily in Michigan, Wisconsin, Illinois, Indiana, and south central Canada. They are, from left to right: (front row) Louis Cato, Eddie Deal, and Ernie Selby; (back row) Germain "Gerry" Bush, Bill Heckman, "Arky" Fenton, Clay Williams, unidentified, and Robert Dewhirst.

On August 30, 1935, before 2,500 fans in Arlington, Nebraska, the City of David beat the Omaha Fords 6–0 to win the Eastern Nebraska Baseball Tournament. The Davids scored five runs in the sixth inning, capped off by a home run by Dick Atwell. Dick Wykoff was the winning pitcher, allowing only one Ford runner to reach third and only three others to advance as far as second. Pictured here are Dick Atwell (left), and Sam Scaling (right).

The City of David arrived in Mexico on September 28, 1935, for an extended barnstorming tour of Mexico. Cecil Tucker, Herman "Flip" Fleming, and Spiesman were not allowed to participate in games since they possessed only tourist passports. Seated is Jesse Lee "Doc" Tally. From left to right, they are: ? Spiesman, Hubert "Hub" Hansen, Herman "Flip" Fleming, Richard "Dick" Atwell, Roy Hutson, John Tucker, ? Clift, Brady, George Anderson, Richard "Dick" Wykoff, and Walter "Dutch" Witte (promoter).

Translated from the poster text, this reads: "The Original House of David a Grand Attraction Worldwide in Baseball and the team La Junta considered actually one of the Best in the Republic of Mexico and the United States of North America." The five-game series was closely contested with the House of David winning two games by the scores of 10–8 and 4–1, while dropping one by a 2–0 count, then loosing both ends of a double-header 3–1 and 2–1.

The City of David ended their season in Paris, Texas, on October 6, 1935, with a 6–1 victory over the local ball team. Harold "Lefty" Daisy picked up the win. Traveling by bus, they covered between 25,000 and 30,000 miles. Their schedule took them into 20 different states, Canada, and Old Mexico. The City of David won-loss record for the season was 146 wins and 50 losses.

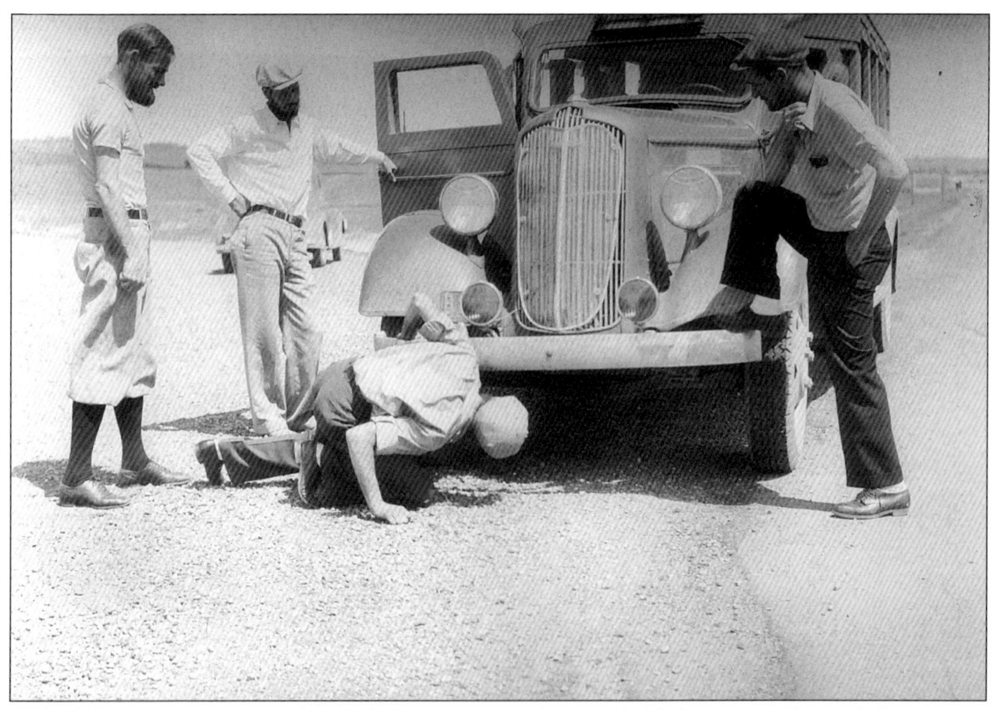

End of the season—end of the road. "We got out of Springfield about 12 miles and the car just stopped. We got towed to Lincoln, Illinois. Wired John; Witte caught a bus for home. John says fix the car. Two days later left Lincoln at 9:30 a.m. Car knocking bad. Arrived home about 4:30 p.m. Sure glad to see everybody!" (Cecil Tucker.)

This photograph was taken on the ferry from Mackinaw. The team buses were also on board. It was the beginning of a Canadian tour for the 1936 House of David Traveling Team. From left to right, they are: (seated) Tony Zitta and Pep Brannon; (middle row) Fred Cato, Eddie Deal, unidentified, and Bob Collenberger; (standing) Dave "Eggs" Harrison, Jim Minogue, unidentified, Lloyd Dalager, Tom Dewhirst, and Matt Collins. Standing at the rear is Tony ?.

In September 1936, the City of David arrived in Hawaii for a month-long stay after traveling over 35,000 miles by car in the U.S., Canada, and Mexico. The Davids played 195 games during the season—losing 46, tying 5, and winning the remaining 144. They are, from left to right: (front row) Al Nusser, Paul "Mickey" Flynn, Roy Hutson, Jesse Lee "Doc" Tally, George Anderson, and John Hubbell; (back row) Harold "Dutch" Witte, John Tucker, Bill Marlott, Cecil Tucker, Don Henry, Fred Cato, Dick Atwell, and Sam Scaling.

The Kansas City Monarchs c. 1936. The House of David/City of David often barnstormed across the country with the Monarchs after their league season ended. Either the Davids or the Monarchs would go into a town to play the locals, followed by the other club's appearance on the next day. They would then conclude their visits by squaring off in a game with each other, much to the delight of the hometown fans.

"We were playing the Monarchs at Yorkton, Canada. The Yorkton manager insisted that the House of David boys honor them by wearing their baseball shirts. The hometown was backing us 100%, until we finally lost the game. Then there were a couple of sore heads who accused us of giving them the game. Anderson accommodated them by saying 'sure, we sold out!!!'" (Interview with former City of David player Fred Larson.)

This picture was taken in 1936 in Stevensville, Michigan. The reason for the visit by Lewis, who did not become World Heavyweight Champion until 1937, is uncertain. However, two years later in 1938, the Champ put together a softball team called the Brown Bombers and returned to the House of David grounds to play an exhibition game at the Colony Park. Lewis played first base on occasion and also coached. He was reportedly sidelined with a sprained ankle for this particular game (something that must have given his boxing manager fits), although the Bombers were still able to come away with a 4–0 victory in a tightly fought contest.

They are, from left to right: (seated) Dave "Eggs" Harrison, Tony Zitta, Lloyd Dalager, unidentified, Eddie Deal, and Hans "Barney" Dalager; (standing) Jim Minogue, Bob Dewhirst, unidentified, Joe Louis, Tom Dewhirst, and Tony ?.

Twenty-one-year old John Hubble (brother of Carl Hubble) was a surprise member of the 1936 City of David team when they arrived in Hawaii (far right, bottom row). A tall right-hander, he pitched the Arkansas City nine to a runner-up position in the National Baseball Tournament in Wichita, Kansas. It was reported that he was offered a contract by the New York Yankees for the next season.

The 1936 Denver Post Tournament began on July 30. Louis Murphy entered his own House of David team in the tournament. Murphy was given instant credibility by hiring former House of David players and tournament participants for his team. Murphy's ball club, however, could not duplicate the success of the 1934 House of David Western Traveling Team and finished far out of the running for the top spot.

Vernon "Lefty" Deck, a hired City of David player for most of the 1930s, had an unusual hidden ball trick. He was able to place an entire baseball into his mouth. Here he is pictured with John Tucker demonstrating this trick—the hard part must have been removing the ball.

"...you know we'd always used to have pepper, play pepper. Hit the ball, pick it, throw it back. They'd hit it back to ya'. Usually three of us lined up when they did that. So we got to juggling the ball around, and passing it back and forth. Actually, the original ones were, on the Pepper Team, myself and Doc Tally, and Dutch Faust." (Interview with George Anderson, June 8, 1991.)

Local St. Joseph sports star Tony Zitta was signed by Rayne, a class B baseball team on March 22, 1937. Zitta was signed because of his exposure and good season with the House of David team during the 1936 season. Pictured left to right are: Tony Zitta, Fred Cato, Bob Collenberger, Jim Minogue, and Matt Collins.

Chicago was always a definite stop on any House of David/City of David road trip. Teams like the Duffy Florals, the Logan Squares, Chicago Carlisle's, the Chicago Union Giants, the Chicago Barber Colts, and Joe Green's Chicago Giants were formidable opponents. Here we see the famous City of David Pepper Team with a member of Chicago's Spencer Coals.

Six

1940–1955

The Twilight Years

This broadside was to have been used to advertise the 1942 version of the City of David ball club. However, before the season ever got underway, Louis Buck (far left) and George Anderson (far right) were drafted into the army. Doc Tally and John Tucker played for the St. Joseph Auto's, and the City of David did not send another team on the road until 1946.

Doc Tally (left) with the original team in 1914, continued his journey on the road until he passed away unexpectedly in 1950. George Anderson joined the Traveling Team in 1927, and continued to play with the City of David until 1956, when the team of bearded barnstormers laced up their spikes for the last time. This added up to a combined 65 years on the road for two of the colony's brightest stars.

Louis Buck was born on July 30, 1914. Originally from Tennessee, he arrived with his parents at the colony in 1916. Louie played on the junior team before joining the City of David traveling team in 1936. His main responsibility for the next four years was driving the team bus and taking care of the gate. Occasionally he would "spell" Anderson at third in the late innings.

In 1942, due to war restrictions, tire and gas rationing, and the military draft of George Anderson, the City of David did not field a team for four years. John Tucker then left the City of David colony to play for the St. Joseph company team, the Auto Specialties. When George returned in 1946, he and Doc Tally reformed the City of David team and took it on the road again.

In the spring of 1943, Jesse Lee "Doc" Tally, having no options to play anywhere else, accepted John Tucker's offer to play for the Auto Specialties team for the 1943 season. Doc continued to play on and off for the Autos until George Anderson returned from the army.

The House of David colony team is pictured here in the 1940s. They are, from left to right: (seated) Taylor Edgell (sponsor and business manager), Eddie Deal, Ernie Selby, Johnny Pavlick, Bill Dudas, George Pavlick, and Bob Farmer; (standing) Lloyd Dalager, ? Adams, unidentified, Harvey Pallas, unidentified, Wilber Ueck, Ike Bohn, and Walt Pierson (umpire).

This team played primarily on weekends and was a member of the Three I league. It also featured a number of players from the area—among them were Ike Bohn. Ike had also traveled with the City of David for a brief period in 1937, and had been a mainstay at shortstop for the House of David home team. Harvey Pallas was a big strong fellow, with an overpowering fastball and a good sinker. Because of his ability to hit for power, he would usually play right field when he wasn't pitching. Johnny and George Pavlick were brothers and were battery mates for the colony team. In August of 1940, John Pavlick hurled a no-hitter against the Conns of Elkhart. He followed this with a one-hit shutout of Kitt's Grocers in September.

In the spring of 1946, The City of David resumed sending out barnstorming teams. This is the 1946 City of David team photograph taken in Kansas City, Missouri. From left to right, they are: (kneeling) George Anderson, Pop Griffen, George Reichelt, Lee Gardner, Richard "Dick" Wykoff, Rocky Kallis, and Jesse Lee "Doc" Tally; (standing) Red Edward, Earl Crappe, Bill Rich, ? Green, Paul "Pete" Jarvis, and Lew Hummel.

The City of David team traveled in two station wagons in the mid-1940s. "On one occasion we blew a tire, and had to be in Portland, Oregon in two hours. So, we hired an airplane to fly the starting pitcher, catcher, and shortstop to the game. The rest of us got the tire on and got to the game in the fifth inning." (Dick Hummel, City of David player.) Pictured here are Doc Tally, Lew Hummel, and another team member.

The 1947 City of David team is pictured here in Oakland, California. The Bearded Barnstormers were still a very popular attraction in 1947, as can be seen by the number of fans that have gathered to watch this ball game. The players are, from left to right: (kneeling) Jack Scott, Sandy Sanders, Bill Horne, unidentified, Lee Gardner, and Earl Crappe; (standing) Dick Wykoff, unidentified, Neil Bryant, Paul "Pete" Jarvis, Bill Mansfield, unidentified, Jesse Lee "Doc" Tally, Al Costello, and Dick Bryant.

May 30, 1934, a federal court handed down a decision that while whiskers may be worn by all and sundry, the name of the House of David may not be appropriated. It found the other teams guilty of unfair competition from which they must cease and desist. It was a moral victory only, however. Some ten years later, Pete Gray is shown in a House of David uniform. He was never a member of any colony team.

Although this photograph is a later version of Paige's All Stars, one thing remained constant, and that was Paige himself. In 1939 and 1940, the City of David barnstormed through Canada and the Pacific Northwest with Paige and his All Stars playing almost one hundred games with them. At one point in '39, the two teams met for 30 consecutive contests. This symbiotic relationship continued into the '50s.

On August 8, 1953, while pitching for the Harlem Globetrotter's Baseball Team, in Seattle, Washington, Satchel Paige pitched two scoreless innings against the City of David. "...George Anderson, the only colony member left on the City of David team, was the player manager, at the time. He and Satchel had been playing against each other for a span of almost 30 years, a truly remarkable accomplishment."

Yes, the House of David also had a basketball team. Formed around 1927, it continued until the late 1950s. The Harlem Globetrotters were frequent opponents as they barnstormed across the U.S and Europe. George Anderson would be with the team from its inception as both a player and later as manager. However, that story is for another book. Players are, from left to right: (front row) George Anderson, Joby Couch, and John Tucker; (back row) Miles Crow and Jesse Lee "Doc" Tally.

During the winter of 1955, after completing the basketball season, George Anderson decided to retire from baseball at the age of 45. The City of David decided not to continue fielding teams due to lack of participation by colony members, thus ending 40 years of House of David/City of David baseball. When asked what he thought had led to the decline in the popularity of "barnstorming" baseball, George's reply was simply, "Television."

Seven

UNIFORM IDENTIFICATION

The original House of David uniform from the time period of 1914–1915 reflected the style that was predominant in the late 19th and early 20th centuries. Dark uniform colors were used, with noticeable collars and high leggings to offset the short pants. The lettering is small, light in color, and arranged in a semi-circle on the upper chest.

As the House of David continued with the team and worked at making this endeavor a money-making operation, they upgraded their uniforms. This uniform was used from 1916–1919. They had the collars removed but still used a dark material. The lettering is still light in color, but is now twice as large as before, more prominently displaying the words, "House of David."

As the modern age of baseball arrived, the House of David was right there keeping with the most current trends. This uniform style was used from 1920 to 1922 and shows the style that was sweeping through the Major Leagues. The House of David adopted light colors with pin stripes. The team name remained in a circular pattern but was now darker than the uniform color.

In 1923, the team changed uniforms and abandoned the circular display of the team name. The subdued HD insignia, seen here, replaced it. It is possible that these uniforms were purchased from another team, and the H was placed over an existing D. They retained the light color with pin striping, but the pants were baggier. The team wore these uniforms until the end of the 1924 season.

These 1925 House of David uniforms used until 1927, kept the pinstripe look and baggy fit. However, they show yet another insignia change. This insignia kept the HD look, but it was placed in an offset position. This insignia is also larger and takes up most of the left side of the uniform shirt.

The team started to make noticeable changes to their uniforms, especially with the unveiling of these 1928 uniforms. The change only affected the uniform shirt, while the pants remained the same pinstriped baggy style. The uniform shirt, however, was not pinstriped, but a solid gray, with a smaller, yet bolder HD insignia. This uniform also utilized piping to accent the button and collar line.

The City of David, after their creation, had the most drastic change to the uniform in 1930. Their style included pin striping and a colorful lapel piping, but in order to distinguish themselves from the House of David, they would use an IHD insignia, with the I being very large and noticeable. This insignia represented "The Israelite House of David, as Reorganized by Mary Purnell." The team wore this uniform from 1930 to 1932.

In the spirit of competition with the City of David for the "Israelite House of David" name, the House of David Home team also used an insignia with an IHD design from 1930 to 1933. A large H with a small D on top, and a small I on the bottom was the insignia. These uniforms were the standard pinstripe with piping to accent the button and collar line.

When the House of David agreed with promoter Ray Doan to franchise the House of David name, he started sending out two teams on the road. In 1933, the Western Travelers utilized a uniform that displayed the House of David name on the shirt in a circle. This was not the only uniform that was utilized in the 1933 season.

With the multiple promotions of House of David teams, it appears they wanted to distinguish each team from the next. Once again, we see the 1933 House of David Western Travelers in full uniform. This style utilized a common theme—a simplistic pinstripe uniform with piping around the button line and collar. In addition, the insignia was a retread of past styles of a large HD on the left side of the uniform shirt.

The 1933 House of David Eastern Travelers wore uniforms that were probably purchased from another organization. The inclusion of an Indian headdress on the left sleeve leads to this conclusion. This uniform did not utilize any pinstripe, but it did have piping for the button and collar lines. Similar to other House of David teams, it utilized an H of D type of insignia.

The 1934 House of David Home team, also known as the Central States Travelers, obtained new uniforms that were a change from their past presentations. This uniform, with lighter colors, had a pinstripe format, but didn't utilize any piping anywhere on the uniform. The insignia was located across the chest with a simple pattern of "H of D."

In 1934 and 1935, the City of David wore the above style of uniform. This uniform continued with the non-pinstripe style, the lapel piping, and the IHD insignia style. However, this insignia was changed to separate the individual letters. The I was the largest of the letters, which indicated the importance of being known as the "Israelite House of David, as reorganized by Mary Purnell."

The 1935 House of David uniform shows a redundant style from past uniforms. This uniform retained the pinstripe style that was so common amongst teams; however, the insignia changed again. This season saw the House of David simply use the letters H and D. Gone is the "I" and the "of" that had adorned past uniforms.

This 1936 uniform, which was used until 1939, did not change much from the previous model. The IHD insignia, with an almost three-dimensional look to it, added greater depth to the uniform. The other change in the uniform was to put more color into the presentation. The letters were red with a blue outline. The piping on the uniform was also blue.

The 1936 House of David uniform pictured in this photograph with Joe Louis is one that was used after the "heyday" of multiple teams criss-crossing the country using the House of David name. This uniform retained the style used by the 1933 Western Travelers, but the lettering was changed to a more gothic style. The return of piping added more flair than in the past. In addition, these uniforms were of a reddish gray color.

This 1940s uniform was a big change for the City of David. Due to WW II rationing, they played more games in the Benton Harbor area, and a BH was placed on their hats to signify that. Their normal insignia is not present, possibly because these uniforms were purchased from another team. Alternatively, it may be that they were required to have a certain style for any inter-league play they may have participated in.

Louis Murphy, as former promoter for the House of David, sent out teams using the House of David name. Headquartered out of Spring Valley, Illinois, these Spring Valley teams were easy to identify by the style of the uniform they wore. The Spring Valley team of 1933 displayed a slanted script lettering style that was never used by either the House of David or the City of David.

Another example of the Spring Valley House of David Team sponsored by Louis Murphy is pictured here. Besides the simple uniform designs, the Spring Valley Team was easy to identify by the posters that always accompanied the team. In particular, the use of the term, "Whiskers, Whiskers," was almost always associated with a Murphy-sponsored team.

Player Lists

The first section of this list includes colony members that played either for the House of David (HOD), or the City of David (COD), or both. The second section details the most comprehensive listing to date of players that were hired by the House of David or the City of David. Players' nicknames are indicated in parentheses after full names. If you feel that any player has been omitted from this list, please contact us via our webpage at www.peppergame.com, our e-mail address at peppergame@peppergame.com, or our PO Box at: PEPPERGAME, PO Box 71, Union, MI 49130.

COLONY MEMBERS

Player	*House of David or City of David*
Anderson, George (Andy)	HOD & COD
Atkins, Tom	HOD
Bauschke, Harvey	HOD
Bauschke, Dwight (Zeke)	HOD
Bell, Leslie	HOD
Bell, Stan	HOD
Boone, J.B.	HOD
Boyersmith, Earl	HOD
Buck, Everett (Louie)	COD
Bulley, Edmond	HOD
Bulley, John	HOD
Bulley, Joseph	HOD
Burland, Elijah	HOD
Caudle, Ben	COD
Couch, Joby	COD
Croft, Hiram	HOD
Crow, Ben	HOD
Crow, Jack	HOD
Crow, Jimmy	HOD & COD
Crow, Miles	HOD & COD
Dalager, Hans (Barney)	HOD
Dalager, Lloyd (Barney)	HOD
Dewhirst, Bob	HOD
Dewhirst, Tom (Bearded Babe Ruth)	HOD
Edmonds, Billy	HOD
Edwards, Amos	COD
Everett, Joe	HOD
Everett, Lionel	HOD
Falkenstein, Charlie	HOD
Faust, Walter (Dutch)	HOD
Frye, William (Bill)	HOD
Hannaford, Ezra (Cookie)	HOD
Hannaford, Horace	HOD
Hansel, Jerry	HOD
Harrison, Dave (Eggs)	HOD
Harron, Jack	HOD
Hill, Benny	HOD
Hornbeck, Estelle	HOD
Hornbeck, Frank	HOD
Jackson, Art	HOD
Jackson, Luther	HOD
Jaft, Ruben	HOD
Johnson, Bert	HOD
Klum, Glenn	HOD
Kolesar, Frank	COD
Link, Billy	HOD
McFarland, Cyril (Mickey)	HOD
Marcum, Richard	HOD
Mooney, Paul	HOD
Moor, Jim	HOD
Nelson, Hobson (Hobie)	HOD
Richards, Curtis	HOD
Sassman, Oscar	HOD
Schneider, Wesley	HOD
Selby, Ernie	HOD
Smith, B.D. (Red)	HOD
Smith, Sidney	HOD
Tally, Barlow	HOD
Tally, Jesse Lee (Bearded Babe Ruth, Doc)	HOD & COD
Tally, Swaney	HOD
Thorpe, Francis	HOD & COD
Tucker, Cecil	COD
Tucker, John (Long John)	HOD & COD
Tucker, Melvin	COD
Tucker, Uber	COD
Vaughn, Hubert (Hip)	HOD
Vieritz, Art	HOD
Wade, Oscar	HOD
Walker, Dixie	HOD
Woodworth, Manna	HOD
Walker, Percy	HOD
Williams, Austin (Tex)	HOD
Williams, Clay (Mud)	HOD
Wilson, Miller	HOD
Wiltbank, Glendon (Red)	HOD
Wiltbank, Leo (Lefty)	HOD
Wright, Billy	HOD
Wulff, Monroe	HOD
Wyland, Frank	HOD

HIRED PLAYERS

Adair, W.E. (Dick)	COD
Adams, Dick	HOD
Agnatic	COD
Alexander, Grover C. (Ole' Pete)	HOD
Ambrose, Elmer	HOD
Anderson,	HOD

Anderson, H.	COD
Andrews,	HOD
Armstrong	COD
Ashman, Dick	COD
Atherton, A.V. (Rip)	HOD & COD
Atkinson,	COD
Atwell, Richard (Dick)	HOD & COD
Ballantine,	HOD
Barnaby	HOD
Bass, Holman (Pee Wee)	COD
Beese	HOD
Bender, Charles (Chief)	HOD
Benson, Al (Bullet Ben)	HOD
Berndt	HOD
Biggers	COD
Bill	COD
Biner	COD
Bird	COD
Birkland	COD
Blackmore, Roy (Blackie, Old Folks)	HOD & COD
Blake	HOD
Blakeney, Buster	HOD
Blastic	COD
Bleeding	HOD
Bohn, Ike	HOD & COD
Boothby	HOD
Bosse, Joe	HOD
Bowers	COD
Brady	COD
Brannon (Pep)	HOD
Bryant, Dick	COD
Bryant, Neil	COD
Burkham, Chauncey	HOD
Bush, Germain (Gerry)	HOD
Bussie	HOD
Bysco	HOD
Caldwell	COD
Campbell, Cecil	COD
Cato, Fred	HOD & COD
Cato, Louie	HOD
Champion	HOD
Chapman, Al	COD
Chavis	COD
Chozen, Mike	HOD
Clay, Clifford (Count)	COD
Clift, Frank	COD
Cofer, Doyle	COD
Coleman, Art	COD
Collenberger, Bob	HOD
Collins, Matt	HOD
Conley	HOD
Cook	COD

Cooke	COD
Corneglia	HOD
Costello, Al	COD
Coykendall, Ed (Koke)	HOD
Crapp, Ted	COD
Crappe, Earl	COD
Crawford	HOD
Croft	HOD
Cross, John (Slick)	HOD
Crotty	COD
Culley	COD
Curtis	HOD
Dacus, Cleo Glenn (Lefty)	COD
Dafoe	HOD
Daisey, Harold (Lefty)	HOD & COD
Davis (1925)	HOD
Davis (1936)	HOD
Deal, Eddie (New Deal)	HOD
Dean (Pa)	HOD
Dean, Elmer (Goober)	HOD
Deck, Vernon (Lefty)	COD
Denaway, Walter	COD
Didrikson, Mildred (Babe)	HOD
Diester	COD
Dodd	HOD
Done	HOD
Drager	COD
Dudas, Bill	HOD
Dunaway	COD
Dunden	COD
Edward (Red)	COD
Eggleston	COD
Egnatic	COD
Elliot	HOD
Ells	COD
Emmer	HOD
Falk	HOD
Farmer, Bob	HOD
Faust, Walter (Dutch)	HOD & COD
Fawcett	HOD
Fenton (Arky)	HOD
Fielder, Ralph	COD
Fine, Johnny	COD
Fish	HOD
Fleming, Herman (Flip)	HOD & COD
Fletcher	HOD
Flynn, L	HOD
Flynn, Paul (Mickey)	COD
Frantz	COD
Freeman	COD
Gardner, Lee	COD
Gebo,	HOD

Gilbert, George (Lefty)	HOD & COD
Gilmore, Joe	HOD
Gordon	COD
Green	COD
Griffin (Pop)	COD
Hackman	HOD
Hagen, Bob	HOD
Hall	HOD
Hall, Howard Thomas (Holly Hall)	HOD
Hamman, Ed	HOD
Hanley	HOD
Hansen, Gene	COD
Hanson, Hubert (Hub)	COD
Hardach	HOD
Hardin	COD
Harding	HOD
Haruska	HOD
Hauser	COD
Hayes, Dick	COD
Hayes, George	COD
Heckman, Bill	HOD & COD
Hendrickson, Don (a.k.a. Henry)	COD
Henny	COD
Henson	COD
Hepting	COD
Hetherly, Clarence W. (Fats)	COD
Hill, Dewey	COD
Hill, Herbert	HOD
Hines, Jimmy	COD
Hipp, A.B.	HOD & COD
Hoffman	HOD
Hoger	COD
Holland, Cral (Jack, Dutch)	HOD
Honus, Bob	COD
Horne, Bill	COD
Houser	COD
Hubbell, John	COD
Hulser	COD
Hummel, Lew	COD
Hummel, Ricard (Dick)	COD
Hunter, Miles Frank (Spike)	COD
Hutson, Roy	COD
Ingram, Mel	HOD
Jackucki, Sig	HOD
Jacobs	HOD
James	HOD
Jansen, Larry	HOD
Jarvis, Paul (Pete)	COD
Jenny	HOD
Johnson	HOD
Johnson, Bert	HOD
Joseph, Billy	HOD

Kafouri, Al	COD
Kafoury, Charles	COD
Kallis (Rockey)	COD
Keller	COD
Kelmer	HOD
Kenney	HOD
Kertis (Lefty)	HOD
Knapp	HOD
Kretchman	HOD
LaBate, Joe	HOD
Lafleur (a.k.a. Laufer)	HOD
Lane	HOD
Larson, Fred (Zeke)	COD
Lauder, Harry	HOD
Lewis (Smoke)	COD
Lick, Eddie	COD
Litfin	HOD
Lofter	HOD
Lorance, William (Red—aka Lawrence)	COD
Lucas, John (Buster)	HOD
Mack	COD
Malek	COD
Mansfield, Bill	COD
Mapels, Rolla (Softball)	COD
Marlott, Bill	COD
Maurer, Gus	COD
McCafferty, Thomas (Mac)	HOD & COD
McCall	HOD
McCarthy, Charles John (Jack)	HOD
McCormick, Frank	HOD
McDougal	HOD
McGraw, John	COD
McKay	COD
McQuillen, Frank	HOD
Mentz	HOD
Miller, Lloyd	HOD
Miller, Louie	HOD
Miner, D.E. (Beans)	COD
Minogue, Jim	HOD
Mitchell, Beatrice (Jackie)	HOD
Moon	COD
Moore, Roy	HOD
Moran	COD
Moulder	HOD
Mullen (Moon)	HOD
Mullis	HOD
Murphy, Art	HOD
Neve, Page	HOD & COD
Newell	HOD
Nickerson, Frank (Bobo)	COD
Noel, Charles (Chuck)	COD
Nusser, Alvin (Al)	COD

Oakeson, Duke (a.k.a. Okeson)	COD
O'Brien	COD
O'Grady, Carl	COD
O'Hara	COD
Oleson	HOD
Olsen	COD
Orwell, Ossie	HOD
O'Shaughnessy	COD
Oster	COD
Paige, Leroy (Satchel)	HOD
Pallas, Harvey	HOD
Pavlik, Johnny	HOD
Pavlike, George	HOD
Pearson	HOD
Pederson, Carl (Cyclone)	HOD & COD
Perkins, Bill (Cy)	HOD
Perry, Mason (Mac)	HOD
Peters, Bill	COD
Pflingstler	HOD
Phelan	HOD
Pike, Williard (Bill)	COD
Pociak, Mike	COD
Popowski, Eddie	HOD
Potter, tony	HOD
Powell, Ray (Skeeter)	HOD & COD
Prince, Victor	HOD
Pugh	HOD
Radloff, Fred (Joe, Windy)	HOD & COD
Rapp	COD
Rathburn	HOD
Ratkowski	HOD
Reed	COD
Reed, Clifford (LaPorte)	HOD & COD
Reichelt, George	COD
Rich, William (Bill)	COD
Richmond, Bob	HOD
Rocky	COD
Rothblatt, Marvin	COD
Rucher	COD
Rutkowski	HOD
Saba, Dick	COD
Salas, Frankie	HOD
Samule, Marvin	COD
Sanders (Sandy)	COD
Sauer, George	COD
Savage, Emery	COD
Scaling, Sam	COD
Schmiegle	HOD
Schroeder, Mike (Lefty)	HOD & COD
Scott, Jack	COD
Sharrock	HOD
Shinonick	COD
Shroder	COD
Sibering, Dick	COD
Siddle	HOD
Smith	HOD
Smith, Chet	COD
Smith, Earl	HOD
Smith, Harold (1925) (Pup)	HOD
Smith, Harold (1933)	HOD
Snell	COD
Speck	COD
Spiesman	COD
Spradlin, bill	COD
Stallard	COD
Steinecke, Bill	COD
Stem, Al	HOD
Susse	COD
Swift	COD
Swinehart, Ossie	COD
Tapley	HOD
Tapsee	HOD
Thenhaus	COD
Tolles, Albert (Lefty)	HOD
Tomski	COD
Traynor	HOD
Trine, Brad	COD
Turk	COD
Ueck, Wilbur	HOD
Vance	HOD
Velcheck, Arnie	COD
Vick	COD
Wagner (1920)	HOD
Wagner (1940)	HOD
Wagner (1949)	COD
Walsh	HOD
Warneke, Al (Young)	HOD
Wegner, Bob	COD
Welmer	COD
Whitehill	HOD
Wierman, Warren (Lefty)	HOD
Williams	COD
Williams, Denny	HOD
Wilson (Ug)	COD
Wisniewski, Ray	COD
Woodhouse	HOD
Wright (Red)	HOD
Wykoff, Richard (Dick)	HOD & COD
Wyson, Dick (Biff)	HOD
Young, Doolittle	HOD
Zaeliers	HOD
Zediker (Bud)	HOD
Zentura, Joe	COD
Zitta, Tony	HOD